Major Donor Game Plan

Rounding 3rd and Heading Home

Patrick G. McLaughlin

Published by:
The Timothy Group, Inc.
1663 Sutherland Dr. SE
Grand Rapids, MI 49508
Email: info@timothygroup.com

Cover Design: Susan Harring
Interior Design: Michelle VanGeest
Cartoon Illustrations: Ron Wheeler

ISBN: 0-9788585-0-6

Printed in the United States of America

To Jane, my dear bride,
thank you for putting up with my crazy schedule for thirty-three years.

To Seth and Matt, my sons, thank you for your understanding;
I missed too many ball games, tennis matches, and band concerts.

To our parents, Betty and Del, and Royal and Mari,
thanks for all of your guidance, support, and prayers.

Special thanks to Dean Galiano with Cook Communications Ministries —
I love you man;
to Jean Bloom with Zondervan Publishing,
and to Sarah Nunham with The Timothy Group,
thank you for your labors of love and all your help and wisdom.

To all of my Timothy Group colleagues, clients, and friends—
thanks for the memories; it has been a joy to serve with you
and meet many of your major and mega donors.

Table of Contents

Preface

Somewhat unbeknownst to me, I have been preparing to write this book and share my story for more than twenty-five years. And you know what...it's been fun.

I have been in the business and ministry of stewardship since graduating from seminary in 1981. And unlike many in the consulting arena, I have been and always will be a field person. Blessed to serve alongside some of the finest church, parachurch, and mega-church organizations in the U.S.A., Canada, and U.K., I make more than two hundred major-donor presentations each year—and I have been doing that for the past fifteen years.

Many years ago I redesigned the "Moves Management" concept, which involves steps for building relationships with major donors, to fit my personality. While the concept did not quite work for me before that redesign, now it works extremely well. I've made requests for special projects and annual, capital, and endowment funding—in person, face to face, often at kitchen tables. I have extensively researched giving patterns, likes and dislikes, and why high-capacity donors give and why they do not.

So I have *been there* and *done that* with major donors of all shapes, sizes, and in a multitude of age demographics, all around the world. What I have to share is not just theory; it is practical and based on real-life experience. Many of you have heard bits and pieces of my story at conferences, in board rooms, in airports, or in cars on the way to donor visits, and the anecdotes in this book came not just from major-donor conversations but also from some of you. And from baseball.

Yes, baseball. Baseball is a microcosm of life itself, and I have been involved in the game since age five. I played through high school, during my college years, and well into my adult life. I have been coaching and umpiring since 1987, currently umpiring more than thirty baseball games every year. As you will see in these pages, the game of baseball and the game of life have some real similarities.

The principles in this book, which are exactly the same for Canada and the U.K. as well as for the U.S.A., will work for you and your organization because they have worked for lots of people just like you. I owe many debts of gratitude to people who have taught, trained, and discipled me over the years, as well as to the fifteen hundred clients who have trusted me, employed me, and practiced what I was preaching. It is in their honor that I pass along these principles with high hopes you will use them and find them valuable.

Now grab a cup of coffee and strap in for a great journey into the world of major donors. I hope after you read this book you'll share it with a friend.

1

It's All about Planning

"If you don't know where you are going,
you are liable to end up some place else."
—Yogi Berra

As I was growing up in Wichita, Kansas, my mother reminded me at least a few hundred times that I would never get a second chance to make a first impression. (Thanks, Betty baby—Mom. I've never forgotten your wise admonition.) Let me share this real-life incident that speaks so pointedly to this truth.

No "Do-Overs"

For many years I have been an MHSAA high school baseball umpire. I try to squeeze in thirty spring and summer baseball games. Why? One simple reason: It's fun. Yes, having coaches, players, and parents yell at me is a lot of fun—most of the time. (You're already thinking there must be a little something wrong with me.)

A few seasons ago on a nice spring day, I was working a high school double-header with my umpire partner. In the second game I had the dish (I was behind home plate), and in the third inning it happened! One out, bases loaded, and the clean-up hitter (fourth batter in the lineup) stepped to the plate for the home team. No names, and you will soon see why. I knew it was the clean-up hitter because the coach from the visiting team yelled to his battery (the pitcher and catcher), "number four stick." The count was one ball and

No "Do-Overs"

one strike, and the right-handed pitcher on the mound hung a breaking ball.

Now stay with me, you non baseball fans. All that means is that the curve ball was not curving. The pitch hung inside and just kissed the right-handed batter, "Number 22," on the last knuckle of his left hand. If the batter would have moved his hands a fraction of an inch, the pitch would have been called a ball with no harm done, and he would have had an opportunity to hit the next pitch. Here is where the story gets interesting and you will see why first impressions are so important.

I raised both hands and stopped the play. "Dead ball, it hit him. Number 22, take your base." The catcher popped up and said what nearly every catcher in America says when the ball hits a batter, "Hey, Blue (we wear blue shirts and caps as umpires so they call us Blue), he's got to try to get out of the way." This is somewhat true. The player can not lean into the pitch, but obviously this player did not intend to get hit. I was fairly certain this player—the clean-up hitter batting with the bases loaded—was at the plate to try to hit a home run. Now, as I have done many times in the

There are no do-overs in life or in baseball...

past, I very graciously explained things to the catcher. He did not like my response but had resigned himself to live with my call.

I noticed Number 22 was still at the plate and had not taken the slow walk to first base as required because the ball had hit him. Once again I said, "Number 22, take your base." As I walked around the catcher, Number 22 looked me in the eye and said, "Sir, my coach sent me up here to hit. Is there any way I could do this over?" After hundreds of games and many years behind the plate, I thought I had heard it all, but apparently not! This poor kid was dead serious.

The catcher who had disengaged from our conversation leaned back, dying to hear my response. In fact, I too was dying to hear my response. I said, "Son, I am fifty years old and am fairly certain there are no do-overs in life or in baseball, but here are your options." Pointing to first base to make sure he remembered where it was, I said, "You can walk ninety feet to first base, or," I said as I then pointed to the dugout, "you can walk back to your dugout. And when you get three feet beyond the chalk line, I am forced to call you out. What would you like to do this fine day, Number 22?"

This player, believe it or not, was not in any hurry. In fact, the kid was so disgruntled about letting the ball hit him that I thought he might actually walk toward his dugout. Finally, he headed to first base, got an RBI by walking in a run, and the game went on.

Just as in baseball, there are no do-overs with your major donors. You will always have options, but there are no do-overs. Their first impression of you and your organization is so very important. It takes a plan to build and enhance any donor relationship, but especially for high-capacity donors. Sometimes the options are not very good and they most certainly are not the grand slam this ball player had hoped for before getting hit by the pitch.

If your first impression is not good, you may never get another chance. There are no do-overs, no second chances for that pristine first impression. Therefore, carefully rehearse your strategy, for you may only get one chance to pitch to that major donor.

Plan Your Work... Then Work Your Plan

Let me share three perspectives on planning. One is from the Old Testament, one is from the New Testament, and one is from —you guessed it— baseball.

King David was planning to hand off the baton to his son Solomon. Here's what he said in I Chronicles 28:19-20: *"All this," David said, "I have in writing from the hand of the LORD upon me, and he gave me understanding in all the details of the plan." David also said to Solomon his son, "Be strong and courageous, and do the work. Do not be afraid or discouraged, for the LORD God, my God, is with you. He will not fail you or forsake you until all the work for the service of the temple of the LORD is finished."* (NIV)

For years I have encouraged organizations to quote these verses to their administration, staff, trustees, donors, friends, and alumni—well, virtually every one of their audiences—with one simple change: Take out the words "Temple of the LORD" and insert the name of your organization. *"He will not fail you or forsake you until all the work for [_____] is finished."* Wow, what a promise. But it doesn't just happen. I believe you must do some planning and understand your plan, just as David did.

Luke 14 is another great planning passage. Luke says in verses 28-30, *"But don't begin until you count the cost. For who would begin construction of a building without first getting estimates and then checking to see if there is enough money to pay the bills? Otherwise, you might complete only the foundation before running out of funds. And then how everyone would laugh at you! They would say, 'There's the person who started that building and ran out of money before it was finished!'"* (NLT)

Major donors want to make sure your plan is sound and that you have truly weighed the cost before you lay the foundation. They want to avoid the risk of your quitting because you ran out of funding. An $8 million donor for a project we worked on a few years ago called me out of an important meeting to ask this question: "Am I about to help this organization start something they cannot finish?" It's a fair question the donor wanted answered before writing a check. Donors are willing to help but they don't want them or you to look foolish in a Luke 14 sort of way. They don't want your organizational plan to be insufficient and their money used unwisely.

> *Too many organizations don't plan to fail...they just fail to plan.*

My third perspective on planning is a very practical one from my favorite philosopher of all time. It's not Socrates, Plato, or Aristotle. It's Yogi Berra, a former All Star catcher for the Yankees. He said, "If you don't know where you are going you are liable to end up someplace else." How great is that advice! Another Yogi-ism, as his quotes are often called, is, "When you come to a fork in the road…take it." Many organizations have been at that fork in the road and, without proper planning, seek God's will and put their plan down on paper, but then find they are heading the wrong way and need to backtrack.

Peter Loose, my dear friend of twenty years, lives in Chelmsford, England. In 1992 Peter invited me to the U.K. to share my stewardship perspective. I have since worked with a variety of churches and parachurch organizations in England and Ireland. On a recent donor visit in Natwich, England, I saw this profound document pinned on the bulletin board outside of an office: *"Planning is an unnatural process, it's much more fun to get on with it. The real benefit of not planning is that failure comes as a complete surprise and is not preceded by months of worry,"* Sir John Harvey-Jones. I do not know Sir John, but he certainly got it right in a tongue-in-cheek, British sort of way.

Too many organizations "don't plan to fail…they just fail to plan." A major-donor strategy will take some planning to introduce, implement, and execute. Everyone from the CEO and trustees to the receptionist will need to buy into the plan and help it become a reality.

Major Donors Ask Major Questions

In 2005 in America, over $250 billion was given philanthropically! America is by far the most generous nation on the face of the earth. Forget what France and Sweden said about U.S. generosity in the tsunami disaster in December of 2004, when they commented that the U.S.A. was giving too little. Canada and the United Kingdom are the next closest in national philanthropy, but the United States is still nearly $190 billion ahead of their combined amounts. Americans are givers.

But major donors ask major questions. That is how they got to be where they are in life and in their business careers. This fact compels organizations to prepare in advance. If you are winging it, donors will know. You will need real, well-thought-out answers, not excuses or "I don't knows."

See how you do with the following questionnaire (see next page). The General Perceptions piece is from the Parker Foundation and is a part of their self-evaluation grant request form. It is a great planning exercise that will help you answer a number of potential major-donor questions up front.

Here are just a few questions we have been asked in the field and point blank by major donors.

1. Are your organizational mission, vision, and core values clear, concise, and compelling?
2. Are you well managed (do you wisely use your time, talent, and treasure)? Does an atmosphere of stewardship exist in your organization?
3. Could you define in simple terms what makes you unique?

General Perceptions

	Strong	In Transition	Struggling	Other
I would characterize our organization today as:	Strong	In Transition	Struggling	Other
Our staff is:	Superior	Strong	Effective	Other
Our financial base is:	Strong	Adequate	Weak	Other
Our funding base is:	Strong	Stable	Weak	Other
Our financial controls are:	Tight	Loose		Other
We have a formal fundraising plan:	Yes	No		Other
Our community support (individual contributions) is:	Strong	Adequate	Weak	Other
In the foundation community, we are:	Well known	Somewhat known	Barely known	Other
In the corporate community, we are:	Well known	Somewhat known	Barely known	Other
In the past three years, the number of clients served has:	Grown dramatically	Remained relatively stable	Decreased	Other
Our facilities are:	Great	Adequate	Inadequate	Other
We are computerized:	In all areas	Few computers	No computers	Other
In the past three years, our staff has:	Increased	Remained stable	Decreased	Other
In the past three years, our overhead has:	Increased dramatically	Remained about the same	Declined	Other
Do you have an individual donor base?	Yes	No	If yes, number on list:	No, who are contributors?

Created by the Parker Foundation.

4. If your organization went out of business tomorrow, who would really miss you (clients, service recipients, customers, donors, etc.)?

5. Do you have a strategic ministry plan that guides your organization? Does it have a price tag attached to it?

6. What would you do tomorrow with an additional $1 million? What would you do with an additional $5 million?

7. Will my (major/mega donor) gift really make a difference to your organization?

8. Will my contribution become a Luke 14 gift, helping you start something you cannot complete?

9. Is your board of trustees active in the leadership of the organization and do they contribute generously on an annual basis?

10. Are your alumni, service recipients, customers, constituency, friends, staff, faculty, and trustees proud of your organization? If yes, why? If no, why not?

If you can answer these questions, you just might be ready to take the next step.

The Game Begins Now...Pre-Season Conditioning

Major donors have no interest in funding the past, and they have very little interest in helping to fund the present. Almost all of the major donors we have worked with have said they want to help purchase the future! An organization with vision, passion, and a real sense of direction for their future has no lack of resources for the planning process. So get ready for the season by "working out" your plan.

Be Sure You Have a Vision and a Strategy

Sometimes organizations do not even get on a major donor's radar screen because the donor's perception is that the organization is just not big enough. Are you worthy of a major-donor gift, or perhaps multitudes of gifts? What does your strategic/advancement/ministry plan call for you to fund over the next one, three, or five years?

Lay out a plan and convert your plan to dollars and cents. We are presently under contract with a Christian college that states a $200 million need over the next ten or more years in their case document. Their initial phase only calls for $32 million of that $200 million big-picture need, but they are letting people know that, when they finish this phase, they are moving to the next phase and the next and so on. They won't discourage any major donors by causing them to believe the need and size of the campaign is too small.

A major donor told me a few years ago that he does not tithe at his church because he thought he would do them a great disservice if he did. He indicated there was very little vision being discussed and implemented by that congregation. He loved the church people and had been there many years, but felt a whole lot more should be happening. He felt they would not know what to do with his money if he gave what he was capable of giving, that it would be an unwise investment of the resources God had entrusted to him.

Although this is not a book about strategic planning, a few additional thoughts here seem appropriate. Major donors will sometimes ask for your "business plan." They just want to know that you have a strategy to get from point A to point Z. Without a sound plan there will be a tendency for major donors to "tip" you—giving well below their potential to merely test you. Ask another self-directed organizational question: "If staffing and dollars were not an issue, what would our ministry look like?" If the leadership of the church previously mentioned had asked themselves that question, if they had been thinking strategically, they could have captured the imagination and passion of this major donor.

The 3 P's of Strategic Planning

In any planning process, address the 3 P's of strategic planning. If we had the money, what would we add in the area of:

❏ *Personnel* (new or re-trained staff).
❏ *Property* (land acquisition, building renovation, new building, etc.).
❏ *Programs* (what new, innovative, or upgraded programs would we address or add immediately if we had the financial resources).

As a general rule, most major donors have a "hot button"—an area of passion—in one of these three areas: new staff, new programs, or new facilities (bricks and mortar). By planning in advance, you can direct donors to their areas of interest as you do your Research or Romance activities. (Research and Romance, as well as the Request, Recognition, and Recruitment make up the 5 R's of the major-donor process. More about these phases in the following chapters.)

Here is a great opportunity to sit down with your staff and create two very important lists. A "needs list" is where everyone shares what they really need to do a better job at your organization. A field person might say, "The DVD/video presentation we have been sharing is outdated. A new one could help me better share our story and enroll donors into one of our giving clubs." Then try to think way outside the box with a "wants list." "If we had money and staffing, what I would want for our organization is a helicopter to take donors on vision tours of our city to share the real and felt needs of our community." Using the 3 P's will surely enhance your planning process, especially with your staff.

...most major donors have a "hot button"—an area of passion...

Early in my career I made a handful of calls to major donors who commented as they ushered me out the door, "Come back and see me when you are ready." In other words, go back home and get your plan together, *then* come back and let's talk. That was very gracious of them. Again, some will remember your lack of planning and test you with their first gift by only tipping you to make sure you do what you say you will do. I cannot stress it enough—clearly, plainly, simply, and concisely lay out your plan. Think, plan, act, and become strategic. Clearly share your vision with all of your donors. Keep in mind that major donors have no interest in where you have been or even where you are. They want to help you fund the future. Become strategic and intentional in all that you do, especially as you share those plans with individuals who have major-donor capacity. Your next step is to determine how to identify and educate major and mega donors to help you fund the plan.

Discover Your "Pat Answers" To These Thought-Provoking Questions

1. Get ready in advance. You only get one chance at a first impression of yourself and your organization. What are the steps you have already taken, and those you need to take?
2. There are no do-overs. Ask the question, "What do we really have the capacity to fund and manage, and how do we put our best foot forward with our major donors?"
3. Ask yourself the tough questions up front. The answers will help you share your story (mission, vision, core values, human needs, and the cost to make it happen).

4. Can you create an organizational "needs list" and a "wants list" with your staff?
5. Are you able to think, plan, and act strategically? It will help you define and share the big picture.

2

It's All about Perspective

If God doesn't build the house, the
builders only build shacks. If God doesn't
guard the city, the night watchman
might as well nap.
—Psalm 127:1-2a (The Message)

Recognizing your perspective on fund-raising is absolutely critical before your organization starts to think
through a successful major-donor program. Do you believe
it's just fund-raising, or is it stewardship? In my mind, fund-
raising is about meeting short-term needs, and stewardship
is a long-term investment. Fund-raising is about giving
from the head (a cognitive decision), but stewardship is
about a decision *from the heart*. Fund-raising has a philan-

thropic feel, and stewardship does not. In some instances fund-raising and stewardship are very closely aligned, but in most instances they represent very different approaches.

A gift from the heart is given for different reasons than a gift from the head. Often, strings are attached to the major gift given from the head. Usually, strings are *not* attached to a gift given from the heart. It's the difference between ownership and stewardship.

Again, I am convinced that your perspective on stewardship is critical! Your understanding of stewardship and your belief system will have a major impact on how successful you are in both the long and short term. Think of a donor relationship as a life-time investment, not merely meeting your annual funding needs or finishing a capital campaign. In my world travels with clients of all shapes, sizes, and needs, I've found four distinct perspectives on stewardship: Those who see it as an element of faith, those who view the process as a necessary evil, those who say it is good because of what it can and does accomplish, and those who see it as a ministry to the donors.

A gift from the heart is given for different reasons than a gift from the head.

Stewardship and the Faith Perspective

Many have practiced the faith perspective over the years, and they will solidly defend this perspective. In fact, some take great pride in saying they have never asked for a gift and yet God continues to meet their needs. Let's apply that perspective to other aspects of our lives. What about these somewhat impractical statements?

- I have never asked for directions anywhere in my life, yet God continues to direct where I am going.
- I have never asked anyone for the time of day, but I am usually on time because God blesses me with being on time.
- I have never asked anyone about his or her faith walk because it is way too personal. Yet I am convinced God will bring that person to Himself in due time.
- God's work done God's way will not lack for God's supply.
- What men and women do with their time, talent, and treasure (money) is between them and the Lord.

If this is your perspective, I hope you will at least give thought and prayer to what I think is a more biblical and practical perspective. A late 1800's orphanage director in England, Reverend George Mueller, is often called the patriarch of this Faith Perspective. George and his staff prayed their knees bare. They asked God to miraculously meet their needs, and quite often He did! They would pray for food, and a milk wagon on the way to market would break down right outside the orphanage. The farmer would bring them the cans of milk, lest they spoil. Similar donations of meat and other foods often came to the orphanage. Please do not misunderstand what I'm about to say; I believe God answers prayer. But I call this perspective the "Mueller Myth."

George and his staff prayed diligently, but when the milk wagon didn't stop and rolled on by, he did something else. He encouraged his staff to sell their earthly belongings and use the money to buy milk and food for the kids. Another time, Reverend Mueller asked three business men to underwrite the cost of rent for a year at a church in Bristol, England, before he would accept the church's call. He wanted to be sure the church was debt-free under his leadership.

But I thought George was famous for never asking, just trusting God! It seems, in his own unique way, he did make an ask or two, and likely many more. I am a fan of George Mueller and deeply respect his life and ministry, but I think careful study will reveal a bit of a twist to this Faith Perspective. Even if you are Mueller-esque in your faith and practice, you may have an opportunity to make a specific ask of some of your key donor prospects or suspects. As you will see in chapter three, Scripture shows us a good bit of personal solicitation activity.

Stewardship as a "Necessary Evil"

Those who view this critical issue of fund-raising/stewardship as a "necessary evil" offer us a second perspective. A large contingent says, "I hate to raise funds, it makes me feel like a beggar, and I truly believe it is an embarrassment to me, our organization, and to the donor. I only do it because my organization makes me raise funds before I can come on staff (or start a new initiative or whatever)." The fund-raising/stewardship process is necessary, but it is viewed as evil—one of those things everyone hates to do but knows they must do.

If you are here, I hope you will prayerfully walk with me and see a different angle. Years ago we worked with an organization that proudly proclaimed "Information with No Solicitation" as one of their organizational core values. They said, "All we do is share information, we do not ask

No "Heavenly Hinting"

anyone in a direct manner to help us. We share the need, hint quite a bit that we need help, and just trust God for the results. We never ask directly. It is always very tasteful hinting, indirect and discreet."

A while back a major donor gave me some of the best advice I have ever received. He said, "Pat, we give to a number of organizations. God has blessed us beyond our wildest imaginations, and we have the resources to bless those ministries." Then he asked me to please pass along this nugget of wisdom. He and his wife came to the conclusion that they were no longer going to give to those organizations that practiced "heavenly hinting." I had been fund-raising a long time, but was not familiar with the term. He said, "We have grown weary of organizations coming to our home, sharing a critical need, and then hinting around about how we could help them. Pat, tell organizations to stop heavenly hinting. If they need money, tell them to be specific and ask us for money. We are comfortable with a specific amount. If they want prayer, have them ask us to pray."

He went on to say they are now limiting meetings in their home to thirty to forty-five minutes. He expected those organizations to make a clear presentation of their case for support, to share a financial need, and make an ask. He said that, in the past, ministry representatives had spent as much as three hours in their home dropping heavenly hints. Appar-

They were no longer going to give to those organizations that practiced "heavenly hinting."

ently they were hoping this couple would finally say, "Well, do you need our money to accomplish this project?" He believes many other major donors are saying "enough," and so do I. Share the need, and then invite people to give generously! Make the ask, then take them golfing, to a concert, or to a ball game to watch their grandchild pitch. You can spend the day with them enhancing a relationship, but the ask itself should only take thirty to forty minutes. It is not a dirty, low-down task to invite a major donor to help you fund your ministry. Those of you who view fund-raising as a necessary evil, please consider another perspective.

Stewardship That Is "Good...Because"

The third perspective on fund-raising is that the stewardship process is good only because of the ministry it underwrites. Now, honestly, I believe this is getting closer to the truth. If this is where you are, I applaud your ongoing efforts. The solicitation process becomes valid because, on the back end of it, ministry happens! The solicitation process becomes valid because your organization is able to accomplish more of your mission. Usually, more money to your organization should mean more ministry. If not, you need to go back to chapter one on planning and review your strategic plan.

The "Good...Because" perspective is valid because, once I raise the money, I get to plant a church in Brazil, build a youth center in Detroit, or open a women's shelter in Los Angeles. The fund-raising/stewardship process is *good because* of the ministry it ultimately underwrites. The end validates the ask. I will be brief with this perspective because it is very close in philosophy to my last perspective—one that I have been practicing and sharing since seminary.

Stewardship as Ministry

I firmly believe that the fund-raising/stewardship process is, in and of itself, a ministry. Stewardship, the philanthropic process, is a way of *serving* people, and a way of serving the donor that allows you to serve more people in and through your organization.

Let me share some information that may persuade you toward this perspective. Whether you are a member of the Association of Fundraising Professional (AFP), a Christian Stewardship Association member (CSA), a Christian Management Association (CMA) member, a CSI, ACSI, or CCCA member, or you're not a member of any national organization, this perspective not only makes sense but can be totally supported with Scripture. Regardless of theology, most of us likely accept the moral and practical aspects of the Judeo/Christian Bible (Old and New Testaments). The Bible is a story of life and redemption recorded through the eyes and lives of mere mortals. Since stewardship (the wise management of our time, talents, and trea-

> *I firmly believe that the fund-raising/stewardship process is, in and of itself, a ministry.*

sure) is a major part of all of the lives of people—past, present, and future—it should be no surprise that the Bible has quite a lot to say on the subject.

Ownership versus Stewardship

Two kinds of people live in the world: owners and stewards. I have met owners who think the money belongs to them, and stewards who know it doesn't. We all work hard to provide for our families and make it in this world. Owners have the notion that they are going to somehow take with them the money they think is theirs. They exhibit the "King Tut" syndrome—"The resources are mine and it is all going into the tomb with me when I die." This perspective surely cannot be supported by either the reality of life or in the reality of death.

I have a dear friend who is also my physician. He and many others in his profession report that, on their deathbeds, people do not want their stockbroker or investment counselor called to their bedside. No, they want their family, neighbors, close friends, pastor, or spiritual advisor alongside them. When the chips are finally down, they realize what really matters is *relationships,* not resources.

My biological father died in 1998 in Joplin, Missouri, from a series of heart attacks. On his deathbed, he asked the ER doctor at St. Johns Hospital to call his children and his pastor. My dad was an owner who thought he was going to take it with him. There was no will, trust instrument, or written plan for his money and assets. In his passing, his five children made stewardship decisions on his behalf. We gave away resources (lawn mowers, tools, TV's, household goods, personal junk) to family and friends to offset taxes, but also because it was the

Two kinds of people live in the world: owners and stewards.

right thing to do. He had a good bit of Wal-Mart stock, but we did not put that into his coffin! It was liquidated and distributed to children and grandchildren. Even owners become stewards at the point of death because someone is going to receive their assets and distribute them. A good bit of my dad's resources went to an attorney, the state of Missouri, and to Washington, D.C., an unfortunate choice he made as an owner who did not plan for his future like a steward. So what does the Bible say about this?

Old Testament Perspective on Stewardship

God created man and then woman in His image. He then placed them into a perfect environment, the garden of Eden. God said to them (excuse the paraphrase license), "Look at all of these cool things I have made. It's all yours. In fact, I made it for you…all you have to do is wisely manage it. Oh, by the way, part of the management/stewardship contract is to leave one tree alone; it is mine. Any questions? Okay, kids, have fun and be good stewards of what I have entrusted to you here in the garden." Well, how did our proverbial parents Adam and Eve do with their first stewardship assignment? Not very well. In fact, the contract was voided and the downhill slide began.

Through the ages, God has entrusted to each of us resources of time, talent, and treasure He wants us to manage in a wise manner to ensure His work here on earth is
accomplished. You see, God does not have a checkbook.
Have you ever seen a check from a major donor written on
the Bank of Heaven? Neither have I. God does His work
through people, and He has blessed some of those people
with significant resources. Let's start with some of those
people in the book of Exodus.

The Tabernacle Campaign

The book of Exodus tells us about the first capital campaign recorded in Scripture with the narrative of Moses'
sharing the need to build a mobile worship center—The
Tabernacle! Moses and Aaron began the campaign by
speaking to those who can share gifts of gold, silver, and
bronze. Exodus 25:1-3 says, *"The LORD said to Moses, "Tell
the people of Israel that everyone who wants to may bring me
an offering. Here is a list of items you may accept on my behalf:
gold, silver, and bronze."* (NLT) Moses and Aaron made an
important stewardship decision. They were directed by
God to speak to major donors first. Everyone participated
in the campaign, but they started at the top and worked
down. This practical, biblical principle is often ignored in
fund-raising projects.

The "Tabernacle Campaign" was so successful that by
Exodus 36:6 they closed off the giving: *"So Moses gave the*

command, and this message was sent throughout the camp: 'Bring no more materials! You have already given more than enough.' So the people stopped bringing their offerings." (NLT) Wow, think about that. The campaign was so successful that Moses and Aaron told the children of Israel to stop bringing their gifts! "Enough, we have more than we need to build the mobile worship center," they said! Conduct your next capital campaign in an Exodus 25 style, using gifts from every category but starting out with high-capacity donors.

Nehemiah and the King Artaxerxes

Let me illustrate and emphasize a well-known and well-researched factor in working with high-capacity donors with a great OT book of Nehemiah narrative about a major-donor request. *It's all about relationships.*

King Artaxerxes was the Bill Gates/United Arab Emirates oil tycoon of his day, and he was wealthy, all-powerful, and his word was absolute law. He was feared by both his own countrymen and the Jews held in captivity. Yet, this Jewish captive, Nehemiah, made a request of Artaxerxes, one of the highest capacity donors in the world.

Nehemiah was the kitchen steward who worked very closely with the king and queen. He hired and fired the cafeteria employees and managed the food services for the entire palace at Susa. The easiest way to kill a king in that time was to poison him. If you could con, manipulate, or bribe a kitchen steward, you might be successful. It is my humble opinion (as a seminary graduate and OT major who has studied the Scripture pretty hard) that Nehemiah was a very heavy guy. If the king got hungry in the middle of the night, he'd wake up Nehemiah to prepare a snack and have Nehemiah eat first to make sure the food was not poisoned. I think they became close pals in their late-night snack runs (no McDonalds with a drive-up window for chariots open until 2 a.m.). During those moments the king wasn't running the country, having people beheaded, or planning his next conquest. It was just two guys munching on cold lamb and pita sandwiches and discussing things like family, sports, and the weather. Nehemiah built a relationship over the twenty years he faithfully served Artaxerxes.

Through a friend, Nehemiah got word that the walls and gates of Jerusalem were still in ruin from a previous campaign against Judah. He was so grieved he began to fast and pray. Then it happened. He was called in to serve the king and queen a meal. Nehemiah knew this Gentile king was the only person who could help him fulfill this call of God in his life to rebuild Jerusalem. The burden was so heavy upon his heart as he began to serve food to the king that his friend Artaxerxes noticed his long face. The king asked Nehemiah why he was sad, opening the door for Nehemiah to share the need and ask one of the most powerful major donors in the world for help. He made his presentation to both the king and queen (great point for you to see husband *and* wife almost always together in a major-donor request).

Nehemiah made four requests of the king and queen:

1. Time off work—a long leave of absence (at a personal risk for the king!)
2. Safe passage between countries with a letter from the king
3. A large supply of timber from the king's forest
4. Some of the royal craftsmen, horses, and guards to help with the project

The king and queen said yes, and so began a journey that would result in the walls of Jerusalem being rebuilt with resources from a Gentile king. Nehemiah organized many of the local workers who helped in the rebuilding process. It was a coming together for the entire nation of Judah! Nehemiah had had the one and only relationship that could help pull off a project of this magnitude.

God has entrusted to each of us resources of time, talent and treasure.

A Major Lesson from a Minor Prophet

The book of Haggai is one of the most misunderstood and under-appreciated books in all of Scripture. Here is a great question (and please, be honest): When was the last time you heard a great sermon on the book of Haggai? Or when was the last time you even heard the book *mentioned* from the pulpit? A long time, I bet—if ever! This minor prophet has been ignored because his message is short, sweet, and right to the point. I often say Haggai is in the "clean part of your Bible." It is not all dog-eared like James or Romans or one of your other favorite study books. I encourage you to take a good hard look at Haggai. Relax, it has only thirty-eight verses. Even if you are a slow reader, you can read it from start to finish in five minutes.

Here is a brief overview of this powerful narrative: Fifty thousand Jewish captives have been released from captivity and return to Jerusalem. They quickly get back into the swing of things—new business ventures, new housing projects, marriage, births, deaths...you know, life. The temple, however, still lies in ruin from one of the past conquests, probably the Hittites or one of those "ites." God wants to get their attention, and get it fast. Who does He use? An eloquent priest or a local business executive with a hot-selling new book? No way. He uses a shepherd! Haggai begins to preach and share a very difficult message: "Hey gang, Jehovah ain't going to bless us unless we stop what we are doing and rebuild His house." The local economy was very strong and people were making money and growing lots of crops, but it just was not working. They were all hungry, tired, and broke because God was trying to get their attention.

Read the sage advice in Haggai 1:5-11 from this inspired prophet. *"This is what the LORD Almighty says: Consider how things are going for you! You have planted much but harvested little. You have food to eat, but not enough to fill you up. You have wine to drink, but not enough to satisfy your thirst. You have clothing to wear, but not enough to keep you warm. Your wages disappear as though you were putting them in pockets filled with holes!*

"This is what the LORD Almighty says: Consider how things are going for you! Now go up into the hills, bring down timber, and rebuild my house. Then I will take pleasure in it and be honored, says the LORD. You hoped for rich harvests, but they were poor. And when you brought your harvest home, I blew it away. Why? Because my house lies in ruins, says the LORD Almighty, while you are all busy building your own fine houses. That is why the heavens have withheld the dew and the earth has withheld its crops. I have called for a drought on your fields and hills—a drought to wither the grain and grapes and olives and all your other crops, a drought to starve both you and your cattle and to ruin everything you have worked so hard to get." (NLT)

Wow, Haggai the shepherd had a very tough message to share with the nation! It seems he was not at all concerned about being politically correct. Haggai began to preach and God began to bring judgment upon the nation. As often happened then and still does today, the people left Jehovah out of the picture. But not for long; Haggai got the political, religious, and social sub-cultures together, and in six months they rebuilt the temple. God was so pleased with them He promised to bless them and protect them (2:19). Jehovah even promised to present them to other nations as a signet ring (a beautiful piece of jewelry), as one of His favorites, because of their stewardship and temple re-building project (2:23). Do you want to please God in your life, in your work, and in your ministry? Work hard, play hard, preach and teach hard, and be a wise and generous steward of your time, talent, and treasure. God will honor you in those difficult tasks. In fact, He will show you off as His signet ring!

In chapter three of another Old Testament book, Malachi, God once again gets very specific and very possessive with His people and their resources. Again, speaking through the prophet, He makes these statements in verses 6-10: *"I am the LORD, and I do not change. That is why you descendants of Jacob are not already completely destroyed. Ever since the days of your ancestors, you have scorned my laws and failed to obey them. Now return to me, and I will return to you," says the LORD Almighty. "But you ask, 'How can we return when we have never gone away?' Should people cheat God? Yet you have cheated me! But you ask, 'What do you mean? When did we ever cheat you?' You have cheated me of the tithes and offerings due to me. You are under a curse, for your whole nation has been cheating me. Bring all the tithes into the storehouse so there will be enough food in my Temple. If you do," says the LORD Almighty, "I will open the windows of heaven for you. I will pour out a blessing so great you won't have enough room to take it in! Try it! Let me prove it to you!"* (NLT)

Want revival in America? Get people giving! Do you want God to really bless you personally, professionally, and in your respective organizations? Become a generous giver. Back to the Malachi passage, we no longer pay our priests,

pastors, or clergy in sides of beef and vegetables, so let's bring it forward to the present day. We need to be generous stewards of all that God has

Want revival in America? Get people giving!

entrusted to us. If we want God to be generous and bless us, according to Haggai and Malachi, we need to be generous to Him. Stewardship is a two-way street.
Last year in America, giving to the local church continued to decline to somewhere between 2-6 percent of joint family income. If the benchmark is the tithe, a gift of ten percent of our total income, we fell way short.

Many major donors have made this comment to me: "We have been very generous over the years with our financial resources, but no matter how big our shovel was, God's shovel was bigger! As we shoveled financial resources that God had blessed us with out the back door, to our church and favorite charities, God continued to bring it in the front door." In essence, they were saying you cannot out-give God. Those two minor prophets, and practical experience, confirm this immutable fact. You would do well to practice Malachi 3:10b, "*Try it [me], let me prove it to you.*" (NLT)

New Testament Perspective on Stewardship

If Jesus pastored your church or my church, every third time He stepped into the pulpit we would hear a sermon on the wise use of our time, our talents, or our treasure.

Yes, we would hear a sermon on stewardship. Yet, in many churches in America, Canada, and the U.K., we hear it once a year, if that! Upon that annual occasion, pastors get up and apologize all over the place for having to preach that day on the touchy subject of giving. I even had a pastor say to me as we began to discuss our *Stewardship Life* program with him, "I have not preached on giving in the past five years, and yet we have hit our giving budget numbers every year at this church. Isn't that great?" How would you respond? I wonder what would have happened—or could have happened—if he had preached and taught the biblical principles of stewardship?

The Old and New Testaments have 1,189 chapters with 31,163 verses. Around 2,300 verses in the Old and New Testaments concern money, materialism, and stewardship. That's 7.4 percent, a bunch for a book primarily about redemption! According to a variety of sources, 1,441 verses just in the New Testament clearly address or touch on the areas of stewardship (money, materialism, time, talent, and treasure). The New Testament has more verses about stewardship than the 550 verses on prayer and 680 verses on love combined (1,230). Be honest, have you heard more sermons over the past ten years in your local worship center on love and prayer or on stewardship? You have it right, we often avoid the subject of calling people to repentance in the area of how they earn, spend, invest, and give their money. What would Haggai or Malachi say to us if either was a guest speaker for the next three to four weeks in our local church?

In Luke 19, Jesus confronted a very wealthy tax collector in the city of Jericho. His name was Zacchaeus and he was a short guy. I totally relate as I am 5'9" and my partner of many years, Dr. Howard Nourse, is exactly one foot taller than me. When we have worked together over the years, our line has always been that one of us played basketball at Ohio State University and was an NCAA champion, and one of us played point guard for a small Christian college in Iowa. Take a wild guess, who played where? Howie would not need to climb the tree in Luke 19:4, but I, like the tax collector, would need the higher vantage point to fully experience the sermon Jesus was sharing. As Jesus walked by with the crowd, He beckoned Zacchaeus to come down from the tree. Jesus planned to spend the weekend at Zacchaeus's home.

None of the Gospel accounts give us details of the events that weekend, but Zacchaeus, a major-donor prospect living in Jericho, makes a major life-changing and stewardship decision. In Luke 19:8, Zacchaeus states publicly that *"I will give half my wealth to the poor, Lord, and if I have overcharged people on their taxes, I will give them back four times as much!"* (NLT) He agrees to pay back to people four times what he stole from them. That is a lot wiser use of money than in the stock market and our new millennium investments!

Bill Hybels is quoted as saying, "The heart is the easy conversion, but the checkbook is the difficult one." That is no more evident than here in Luke 19. The walls fell twice in Scripture, once in the Old Testament and here again in the New Testament. Both were miracles. One was about the wall around the city; here it is about the wall around the heart and checkbook of the major donor Zacchaeus. The hard shell around his heart fell as he made a decision to follow Christ, and in doing so he became a generous steward. By the way, I believe being a disciple and being a steward are connected. Show me a true disciple, and I will show you a steward. Show me a steward, and you will almost always find a disciple.

The Apostle Paul Practices Stewardship

Paul, the Damascus Road convert who penned much of the New Testament, went through three key phases of his life and ministry relating to stewardship. Keep in mind that Paul was not shy about sharing perspectives from his life and ministry. Nor was he shy in challenging people around him to generous levels of commitment and, in particular, stewardship. Paul considered God his primary resource, not major donors or individuals of any giving capacity. Sometimes he had more than enough, and other times he was cold and hungry. First, he went through a phase when he let no one but God know his needs (a George Mueller approach). In his second phase, Paul worked very hard to provide for his own needs through his own paycheck. And in his last phase, Paul very clearly asked those he knew, or those who knew him, to help financially.

Philippians 4:10-12 clearly defines this George Mueller phase of Paul's life. It reads, *"How grateful I am, and how I praise the Lord that you are concerned about me again. I know you have always been concerned for me, but for a while you didn't have the chance to help me. Not that I was ever in need, for I have learned how to get along happily whether I have much or little. I know how to live on almost nothing or with everything. I have learned the secret of living in every situation, whether it is with a full stomach or empty, with plenty or little.* " (NLT) The context of the passage is Paul's thanking them for their gifts in the past, and informing them that he knows how to get along with much or little. While he appreciates their financial participation in the past, he lets them know that, in this phase of his life and ministry, his dependence is entirely on God's provision.

Using his own personal earnings to be a self-supporting missionary is Paul's second phase. Remember when Paul was Saul? He was an attorney and also had some tent-making and mending skills. Paul knew what it was like to work a real job and to invest that money in his ongoing ministry. Acts 20:34-35 reads, "*You know that these hands of mine have worked to pay my own way, and I have even supplied the needs of those who were with me. And I have been a constant example of how you can help the poor by working hard. You should remember the words of the Lord Jesus: 'It is more blessed to give than to receive.'*" (NLT)

Paul was a tireless worker in all aspects of his life and ministry. He set up his tent-making and repair shop in Ephesus for at least three years and personally discipled a young believer named Timothy. Paul further states in I Thessalonians 2:9b, "*Night and day we toiled to earn a liv-*

ing so that our expenses would not be a burden to anyone there as we preached God's Good News among you." (NLT) Paul worked hard and helped to support himself.

In the third phase of Paul's life and work he made his needs known and asked those with ability to help financially. Paul asked a well-known major donor of his day to help a sister church in need. Paul knew the folks in Corinth had money, and the church in Jerusalem was being persecuted and starved to death by the Roman government. While Paul clearly practiced the aforementioned perspectives on fund-raising/stewardship, it is a misconception to think he only shared his needs with God. We have ample evidence that Paul made his needs known to area churches, men and women, and in particular major/mega donor prospects. Some folks in Corinth had plenty of money, and Paul very clearly asked them to give. He was not shy, and there is no reason for any of us to be shy either. It is okay to ask, it is appropriate to ask, it is biblical to ask, and it is practical to ask. I personally believe many of you are missing out with major donors because of your "fear of the ask."

> The heart is the easy conversion, but the checkbook is the difficult one.

Maybe your organization has been and is going through the three phases above, just like the apostle Paul. You have prayed your knees bare, asking God to bring in the funds. You have worked very hard, and in many instances, invested your own funds in the process. Now it's time for many of you to take that next step and very clearly ask. No embarrassment or heavenly hinting, just a straightforward request for the financial partnership of your major-donor prospects and suspects. I think you will begin to see your organization funded in ways you did not think possible. Paul obviously knew what he was doing.

We can learn more from the New Testament. Major-Gifts Officer Paul, with his newly discovered major-gift talent, shared a key stewardship principle with a young pastor named Timothy. He recruited, taught, trained, and discipled Timothy, and then he admonished him to share those truths with others. II Timothy 2:1-2 reads, *"Timothy, my dear son, be strong with the special favor God gives you in Christ Jesus. You have heard me teach many things that have been confirmed by many reliable witnesses. Teach these great truths to trustworthy people who are able to pass them along to others."* (NLT) I founded The Timothy Group in 1990 based on this unique relationship Paul shared with Timothy.

One of the most significant passages in the New Testament on giving is similar to Haggai, and it too gets little pulpit time. Paul and Timothy hung around together for at least three years and built a solid house-church ministry in Ephesus. They were good friends; in fact, I believe they were very close friends. Paul, a strong-willed and sometimes self-sufficient servant, was lonely and cold. He asked his dear friend Timothy to visit him very soon and bring his coat that he had left in Troas (II Timothy 4:13). Once again Paul was in jail, and he missed the fellowship with his young disciple. Paul closed his first letter to his friend and ministry partner Timothy with a great three-point job description for members of that upstart house church in Ephesus. I Timothy 6:17-19 reads, *"Tell those who are rich in this world not to be proud and not to trust in their money, which will soon be gone. But their trust should be in the living God, who richly gives us all we need for our enjoyment. Tell them to use their money to do good. They should be rich in good works and should give generously to those in need, always ready to share with others whatever God has given them. By doing this they will be storing up treasure as a good foundation for the future so that they may take hold of real life."* (NLT)

Allow me a seminary moment and to wax exegetical about Paul's significant admonition to Timothy. First in the three-point job description was this: Tell them to do good, to be about the moral goodness of God. He informed Timothy and the house church that they needed to pursue holiness. You be holy because I am holy and present yourself as "holy living sacrifices" (Romans 12:1). The word *holy* is used 635 times in the Bible, so we can infer that this is a pretty important concept.

The second strong recommendation made in this passage to those early church saints was for all of them to be "rich in good works." Faith without works is dead (James 2:26). Paul says to those members and Pastor Timothy, "Show the town of Ephesus your faith and commitment by doing good works. Practice the great commission and the great commandment. Go reach others with the good news of the gospel and love your neighbor. By doing this you will become rich in good deeds." This is certainly a concept we need to practice today in our lives and faith walk.

The third imperative in this passage is a unique study in stewardship. Paul writes, "that they be generous, willing to share with those in need, the resources that God has entrusted to them." Now, this was a first-century house church that did not have a full-time pastor, youth pastor, or music minister. They did not even have a weekly chariot ministry (going out into the community to pick up children for Sunday school; you know, the first-century bus ministry). In spite of this apparently low-budget church project in Ephesus, Paul was very clear that they needed to be generous, financially willing to share. Why, you ask? So that they may lay up treasure in heaven and take hold of the Christian life.

Now I admit it sounds a bit like a fund-raiser talking, but Paul is very clear that, in giving, we admit and show our trust in God. When I give, essentially I say to God, "Hey, it's Yours. I am just reallocating some of the resources You have entrusted to me to manage." Remember, none of us are owners. There are no U-Haul trucks in funeral processions. So is it okay to ask people to give? According to Paul, we are commanded to do so! Don't be afraid to share with your major-donor prospects an opportunity for a worthy investment in God's kingdom. Invite them to make an eternal investment, one that will bring them closer to God's value system.

I got a bit long-winded in this chapter, but I believe

perspective is a part of the fund-raising/stewardship process that is so often overlooked. Working with major donors, in fact all donors, is *all about relationships*. The Bible is a book that is *all about relationships*.

I hope you understand and clearly see that your perspective on stewardship, people, and relationships will have a major impact on your success as a

There are no U-Haul trucks in funeral processions.

stewardship officer. Money is a unique by-product of building and enhancing relationships with your major/mega donor prospects and suspects. Your planning and perspective on these issues will significantly impact your performance, more than you'll ever realize.

Discover Your "Pat Answers" To These Thought-Provoking Questions

1. Do you really believe any perspective on fund-raising/stewardship will be effective for you and your organization with your major donors?
2. Is it really okay to ask people to give? (Not just hope they will give. Hope is not a strategy.)
3. What is the fundamental difference between an owner and a steward?
4. Was Moses right in seeking the big gifts first (gold, silver, and bronze) in soliciting for the Tabernacle Project? Do you think people were offended that he started at the top and not at the bottom?

5. Can you relate to the apostle Paul, and have you been through his three phases of the stewardship process?
6. Do you believe "it's all about relationships?"
7. Are you ready to make a personal, up-front ask to your top ten major donors?

3

It's All about Research

*Life must be understood backward, but
it must be lived forward.*
—Soren Kierkegaard

Research is the first of the 5 R's, five phases upon which
we have constructed our major-donor game plan over
the past twenty-five years. I'll carefully unpack each of
them—Research, Romance, the Request, Recognition, and
Recruitment—and show you how to make this game plan
work in your organization with your major/mega donor
prospects and suspects.

The Research phase of your major-donor program
is two-fold, internal and external. *Internal* research is an
expansion of your strategic-planning process, where you

clearly define the project, cost, time lines, etc. Your internal research will also involve recruiting and training your team, helping them to understand and build capacity to share with passion your organizational need and case for sup-

The Five R's

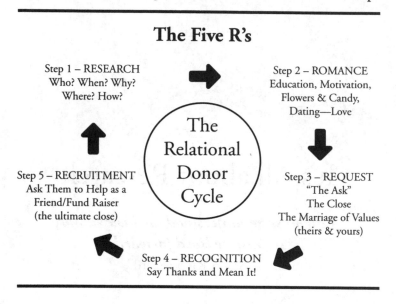

Step 1 – RESEARCH
Who? When? Why?
Where? How?

Step 2 – ROMANCE
Education, Motivation,
Flowers & Candy,
Dating—Love

The Relational Donor Cycle

Step 5 – RECRUITMENT
Ask Them to Help as a
Friend/Fund Raiser
(the ultimate close)

Step 3 – REQUEST
"The Ask"
The Close
The Marriage of Values
(theirs & yours)

Step 4 – RECOGNITION
Say Thanks and Mean It!

port. *External* research is gathering as much information about the major-donor prospect as possible before your first visit. In doing so you will determine if your first visit is one of Research and Romance or if there is the possibility of making a Request on the first visit.

Art and Science

Gathering research is both art and science. The art of working *through* people who know the major-donor prospect or suspect is very important. Close behind is the science of gathering information, and in our information age you can gather a good bit of information from a variety of sources. The Internet has made all of us sources of information. It you don't believe it, enter your name on Google and do a search on yourself. You may be surprised what you discover! If you have published an article, are a member of an association, or have been named in a newspaper article, you will find some personal information about yourself on the World Wide Web.

If I had to select one over the other, I would choose art over science since people are a great information source. They can provide information all the scientific data in the world just cannot provide. The Millionaire Next Door series of books makes it clear that some people live beneath the radar and all the "hard asset" research in the world will not provide much information.

Rudyard Kipling said, "I use five strong men to help me tell a story: who, what, when, where, and why." That is a good starting point for some basic research. Begin by asking the most basic questions about a major/mega donor prospect.

- Who is this person—*really?*
- What is his or her area of interest for giving (personal hot button)?
- Does this person like to give monthly, annually, calendar year end, etc.?
- Does this person like to give to capital projects (bricks and mortar) or annual/operational needs?

- Is this person a candidate for an estate plan or some kind of unique tax impacted gift (property, stocks, etc.)?
- Where does this person live and work?
- Where do his or her resources come from (the market, an inheritance, a thriving business)? Is it old money or new money?
- Why do you think this person might give a gift to your organization?

I admit it seems rather basic, but this is a great starting point in your research. You are beginning the process of getting to know your major-donor prospects.

Begin with an "inside out" perspective. Start close to home, with those you already know. Your current donor file is a great place to begin both your art and science research, and some in-depth research of your current donor file is very important and revealing. It is quite common for organizations to be unaware of potential major donors already on their current mailing lists. Zip code analysis can easily tell you where people live, which is a good thing to know, but it may not tell you the whole story. You will know how much the homes in the neighborhood cost, but it does not necessarily tell you anything about capacity. Careful study of the book *The Millionaire Next Door* by Dr. Thomas J. Stanley and Dr. William D. Danko will reveal that people who live in gated communities do not always have big money. Sometimes they have big mortgages. The book provides a good bit of sage advice, such as not judging a book by its cover. If a family makes $600,000 a year and spends $650,000, it's a fair assumption that trouble may be looming. They most likely are not good major-donor prospects.

We are currently working with a client on a capital campaign. The organization has 60,000 names on their donor file and 35,000 of them are active, which means they have given in the past eighteen months. We are going to research approximately 3,000 names, however, to gather a major-donor list of around 300-500 names for major/mega donor consideration. Many organizations feel they can manage about one hundred major-donor relationships on an annual basis. With a major-donor committee/team (trustees and volunteers) helping with the research, we have a capacity to manage a larger number of major-donor prospects and suspects. Because this

Gathering research is both art and science.

project is a capital campaign, we will assign a number of these names/relationships to a close acquaintance or a business associate to make the (Research, Romance, or Request) personal visit. Yes, with good research, some good coaching and mentoring, your board and key volunteers can assist you greatly.

The science portion of your plan is to use an outside information gathering service to help you understand your major-donor prospects' ability and capacity. If your organization is like most nonprofits, you really don't know much about the people on your mailing list. An asset screening of your data base will typically identify 5 percent of your constituents as potential major donors. Again, most nonprofit organizations are surprised to uncover affluent prospects they didn't even know existed!

Several companies offer services that match constituents from your mailing list with wealth-indicating databases. These data sources have public information that identifies executives of privately held companies, insiders of publicly traded companies, and individuals who own income producing assets such as apartment complexes and strip malls. Other data available includes private investors who have active investment portfolios, individuals who own residences with assessed values of over $1 million, and people who own luxury assets such as yachts and personal aircraft.

The sources of data include publicly reported directories that list physicians, attorneys, architects, engineers, and financial planners. All political donations are public record and can give you insight into a prospective donor's point of view. Biographies listed in *Marquis Who's Who* are extremely accurate because the person listed supplied the information. Often the entry reveals educational background, church affiliation, volunteer positions, family information, and hobbies and interests.

Asset screening is a great tool in your donor Research process, but it doesn't tell you everything about a prospective donor. The value of asset screening is not that it provides a complete financial picture but that it flags an individual for further research. You will have to do additional research before determining an individual's full potential. Asset screening takes your mailing list that looks like a phone book and turns it into the top one hundred donors to visit first in your campaign.

The Major/Mega Donor Research Team

Okay, so now you have gathered some initial information and discovered there may be some major/mega donor prospects out there. You know how much money you need to raise, and you have some idea of who you think may fit your major-donor profile. Now you need a major-donor Research team.

Research is way too big to do by yourself or with a very small staff. As you begin to build capacity for a major-donor program early on, recruit and build your major-donor team. "Many hands make for light work" says a proverb, and it is certainly true as you begin to research potential major-donor prospects and suspects *Begin with an "inside out" perspective.* in your community. Your team is composed of key staff members and key volunteers to your organization. Others who could help in the Research process are local and national major donors. Yes, it is no surprise that your major donors know and spend time with other major donors. Your local banker, trust officer, and even a CPA/tax preparer could be very helpful in this endeavor. A good CFP (certified financial planner) or life, property, and casualty insurance agent could be a very effective member of your team. Your town or city has an attorney whose major practice is estate planning. Attorneys are often great friends in the Research process. They certainly know the old and new lines of money/wealth in your neck of the woods. This information can be very helpful in the Research portion of your major gift effort.

Old and New

Old money is financial wealth that has been around your city, town, or neck of the woods for twenty-five years or more. New lines of money in your area or region are wealth that has been accumulated in the past ten to fifteen years. Identifying those old and new lines of money is a very worthwhile exercise. Ask your major-donor team to help you identify those resources and then discuss who the decision-maker is for those funds. Sometimes it will be a family foundation and a group of family members will vote on your request. But often it is simply an individual or a couple who will sit down and review your proposal and make a decision. Part of your research is to identify these pools of resources and discover who knows them and can become an advocate for your organization.

A number of years ago in Memphis, a major donor (old "blue blood" money) said this to me: "Sir, I do not know you, The Timothy Group, or the organization for which you are making this request. But I know this man (the major-donor volunteer who took me on the call) and I knew his daddy. In fact our families have done business together for over forty years, and if he believes this is a good investment of our hard-earned dollars, then we will give the amount you requested." The beauty of the personal visit was the volunteer making his impact with the major donor. "Do you really believe you can bring all of the churches in Memphis together to accomplish this goal (African American, Anglo, Hispanic, Asian, etc.)?" the major donor asked the volunteer. This regional crusade had the goal of involving everyone from Baptists to Buddhists. Someone on your research team will have a personal relationship with the decision-makers in your city, those with old and new money at their disposal.

I am working in Florida this week as I write this chapter. It should come as no surprise that old money in central Florida is from agricultural and phosphate. Citrus and mining were the old money, looking back across the business landscape over thirty years ago. Those industries or professions generated the wealth. Do you know what is generating wealth in central Florida today? Ah…how about tourism, family activities, water parks, amusement areas, and entertainment? Kissimmee County has more rental cars than any other county in the world. Part of your research needs to be the discovery of old and new wealth sources you can access for your organization.

Start with your current donors to help you with the *Who* part of your research. Include those who have given to your annual/operational campaigns as well as those who have contributed to your capital efforts. Please, do not forget those who have some type of planned giving instrument on the books. Too often organizations tend to write off those who have named their organization in an estate plan. Your endowment donors may be a key to other donor prospects and suspects. Take a look at lapsed donors—they loved you at one point in the life of your organization. Sometimes it is easier to re-win a former major-donor friend than it is to find a new one. Board and advisory board contacts are great sources of major-donor prospects. Mature stewards you know about in your area are great sources of information. Founda-

> *The value of asset screening is...that it flags an individual for further research.*

tions, corporations, and businesses are good sources to research, as well as parents, grandparents, families of service recipients, and families connected to your volunteers. You probably have plenty of prospects in and around your organization. Just do a little old-fashioned research.

Even if you have a large, productive advancement/development team, your CEO/president *must* be very involved in this early research of major-donor prospects and suspects. In fact, let's get it out there right now. The *chief* fund-raising officer in your organization is your CEO. Why, you ask? Because corporate presidents/CEO's/people of wealth/major donors want to meet, greet, interview, query, and build a relationship with your CEO. While a board or trustee member may introduce your CEO and help you share the story, often the final discussion is ultimately between the two CEO's. It is not just important, it is essential that your president/CEO know and understand his or her role as a key performer on the major/mega donor team.

I have been on donor visits where I made the ask, sharing the amount of money the organization was seeking. But once that was accomplished I was totally out of the conversation as the president of the organization and the president of the corporation/business had a CEO-to-CEO, heart-to-heart chat about money, vision, and funding for the project. We will discuss this further in our chapter on the Request. A final word: If the president of your organization is unwilling to be involved in your major-donor program, your performance and production will no doubt be limited.

My years of experience with the NGO Sector—Non Governmental Organization, the new designation for the not-for-profit 501(c)3 organization—has continually emphasized the importance of the board of directors/trustees. To be successful in the Research, Romance, Request, Recognition and Recruitment (the 5 R's) of major donors you will need your board's assistance.

Does your board of directors have a job description and performance expectation? Does that job description involve their role in the fund-raising process of your organization? If not, why not? Look at this another way. If you have eight or twelve board members, or thirty-six like a college, they can all become members of the advancement/ development/major-donor team. We have re-trained and re-tooled many board members into becoming "fund-raisers" or "friend-raisers." Either way, your trustees take on an entirely new level of ownership in your organization.

We all know it is sometimes difficult to hold your board/trustees accountable to help you recruit and solicit

_____ major donors. But many have

Plan your work, actually enjoyed learning how
then work your to become a "raiser" (friend or
plan! fund). Once a few get rolling
and become productive, they
encourage their colleagues to get going as well.

I hope all of your trustees are donors. I'm not convinced that just because they invest their time or their talent they make great board members. They also need to invest their treasure in your organization. Matthew 6 reminds us "if your treasure is there, so will your heart be also." You want the hearts of your board, you want them to help open doors in your community, and you want them to assist with your major-donor program. Sign them up as donors!

Why Major Donors Give

Extensive research is available on why major donors give, especially for the first time. I hope you are sitting down, because this is going to be a big, earth-shattering revelation. RELATIONSHIPS pure and simple! I know, I nearly floored you with that one. You know it is true through case studies, other books written about fund-raising, and the E.L. Lilly study. And almost every other human relationship study clearly indicates how important relationship is. The major donor knows, loves, or respects someone involved in the Research, Romance, or Request process for the organization seeking funds. In our research with major donors the *cause* was often second or third on their list of reasons to give! Relationship to a trustee, staff member, key volunteer, service recipient, or other major donor involved in the project carried a lot of weight in the decision-making process. As you begin your Research phase, be sure to recruit a handful of major donors or people who know other major donors to assist you. Major donors often give because, during your research, you matched them with a fellow major donor. It is not rocket science. It is, in fact, *all about relationships*. The establishment or enhancement of those relationships begins and ultimately finishes with your research.

A-B-C Rating Is Your Final Research Step

If discovering or developing an existing relationship is the ultimate goal early in the major-donor planning process, here is one additional step. Assign an A, B, or C rating to every donor prospect and suspect. Donor prospects or suspects knowledgeable about you and your organization should receive an A rating. How much organizational information, history, education, and awareness qualifies them for an A rating is a question only you and your Research team can answer. To receive an A rating, donors must know you and you must know them.

Here are some helpful questions to ask about major donors:

- Have you dined with them in the last ninety days?
- Have you been in their homes or have they been in your home in the last year?
- Do you know their children by their first names?
- Do you have their cell phone numbers? Do they have yours?
- Have they ever been asked to give and have they turned you down?
- What does their year-to-date giving record indicate?
- Where (to whom, what causes) have they given in the past ten years?
- What was their largest one-time gift?
- What is their area of passion (i.e., what gets them excited)?
- What is their "hot button" in their giving? Is it operational, capital, or program?
- Do they invest big here at home or outside the U.S.A.?
- Do they get excited about children, mercy ministries, 10-40 window organizations?
- Is evangelism or discipleship their passion?

These are just a few of the questions that will help you identify an A contact.

For a prospect/suspect to receive a B rating the information flow is only one way. You know a lot about them, but they know very little about you. Or they know a lot about your organization, yet you could not pick them out of a crowd. On a recent capital project, I interviewed a mega-donor prospect in his office. It appears this family will make the largest commitment to a $27,000,000 campaign. The initial gift was $2,000,000, which would qualify as a major/mega donor for most organizations. On the pre-campaign/feasibility study interview sheet, key leaders of the organization indicated they would not be able to identify this person if they saw him. They did not know who he was and had never been to his home or office. He knew their organization, but they knew very little about him.

This is a classic example of a B contact. Just a quick update on the organization. They have since visited the mega-donor prospect four times in the last sixty days. They had good reasons for each visit (rather than just becoming pests), and the relationship is getting warmer and deeper by the day. They now know the names of his children and the names and ages of his grandchildren. In the early stages of their donor Research process, this donor family received a B rating, and should have. Now they have an A+ rating.

The chief fundraising officer in your organization is your CEO.

Major/mega donor prospects who do not know anything or very little about your organization deserve a C rating when you also know very little about them. You may know *of* them, but you certainly do not *know* them. They may have heard of your work in the area or have a friend who is a friend or donor to your organization. They have, however, never been a contributor, attended an event, carefully read a piece of your mail, or reviewed a proposal for support from your organization. Education and communication need to flow both ways. You need to get to know them and help them get to know your mission, vision, and core values. We will look at this in more depth in the next chapter as we discuss the Romance process. It often does not take long for a donor prospect to move up the information ladder, with the right cultivation. The C prospect's becoming a B and then an A prospect is very do-able with solid research and a good plan.

Plan your work, then work your plan! This is not profound. It is just simple best practice as you lay the foundation for your major-donor activities. Your perspective on the entire fund-raising process and the quality of your research will have a major impact on your success. Once the Research phase is completed then comes what I think is the fun part, the Romance phase.

Discover Your "Pat Answers" To These Thought-Provoking Questions

1. Have you done donor research in the past? What worked and what did not?
2. If you were asked to identify your top twenty-five donors down to the names of their spouse, children, and grandchildren, could you do it?

3. Which will help you the most with your initial donor research, art or science?
4. Can you name five people right now you would want to serve on your major/mega donor Research team?
5. How would the identification of old and new money sources in your universe help? Do you know more of the old or more of the new, and what does that mean?
6. How could the A-B-C rating process help you identify and qualify some major donors today?

4

It's All about Romance

Romance is one of the most powerful affirmative experiences possible in a marriage.
—Dr. Bruce A. Baldwin

In the song "Some Enchanted Evening" from Rodgers and Hammerstein's wonderful musical *South Pacific*, a handsome plantation owner sings about seeing a stranger across a crowded room, just knowing she's the one for you, and never letting her go so you don't have to "dream alone." And, if you know this musical, you know he does get the girl in the end!

Many organizations hope they somehow will meet a stranger who will write a check and solve many of their annual, capital, and endowment funding needs. This romantic scene works so well on the screen and stage, but it sure will not work with your major-donor prospects and suspects. Yes, examples exist of organizations that have achieved success this way. It is rare, however, and most often a relationship is developed through a good, solid plan of first Research, then Romance (education and cultivation).

It's likely that more words about love and romance have been penned and spoken throughout time than any other topic. On Amazon.com or at Barnes & Noble you can find an amazing volume of literature on love and romance. More verses on love (680) are in the New Testament than on prayer (550). A key part of the initial major-donor relationship-building falls under the description of Romance.

A key part of the initial major-donor relationship-building falls under the description of Romance.

The luck of the draw is not how you discover your major/mega donors. It is not seeing someone for the first time and suddenly it's love at first sight. It doesn't matter how good you look to them or how good they look to you. If you do not get to really know them, they will just "tip" you and your organization. If you do not romance them and build the relationship, it is unlikely that you will see them again. Depending on luck (and good lyrics) for your major-donor meetings will almost always be ineffective and disappointing.

Just as in most long-term marriages, the romance continues to grow throughout the years and the relationship sweetens. It goes from interest, to infatuation, to real, true love. That, in fact, is the ultimate test of a donor relationship. Do not think about a meeting or a visit with your major/mega donors as a one-time date. In marriage terminology, here is the question: Were you proposed to on the first date? Very likely not. In fact, very few of those first-date asks have ever worked out. More likely, it took some candy and flowers, and for some of us a *lot* of candy and flowers! You must think of this relationship like you would a good marriage—much longer term, more like a marathon than a 100-meter dash. Rushing the relationship will "cost you" (literally) in your initial gift and in subsequent gifts. Donors will give below their potential.

Can you imagine the number of requests major donors receive in a year's time? Let me help you out—a ton. A number of years ago, one donor in Wheaton received sixty-five requests by mail alone just in the month of December! The opportunity for donors to participate financially with that many organizations is certainly a reality. But, if the 80/20 rule or even the 90/10 rule is in effect, we must romance and build relationships with these major-donor prospects and suspects to even be considered. Eighty percent of your gift income is given by 20 percent of your donor base, or 90 percent comes from 10 percent of your base.

This should cause all of us to take a good hard look at this Romance process. It also tells us we *must* get to know the top 10 to 20 percent of our donor file if they have the financial ability to help us meet and exceed our annual, capital, and endowment funding goals. To be effective we must become much more intentional. My main man Yogi Berra said it best, "If you do not know where you are going, you are liable to end up someplace else." How especially true this is in the Romance education process with your major donors. You need to have a Romance plan and carefully work it!

Gone are the days when we wake up and read in the paper that an old guy in our community died and left $15 million to an organization that didn't even know him. For the sake of example, let's call this gentleman Clyde Johnsonberger. I have never met anyone by that name so I think it is a safe name to use. You all know his type. A bit of a hermit, lived light years below his financial ability, was extremely frugal, and unbelievably generous. Often more generous in death than he was or at least appeared to be in life. Many of these types of donors are anonymous, very quiet, and often very secret contributors. Clyde drove an old pick-up truck and lived in the same tiny two-bedroom home he had lived in for the past fifty or more years. If you saw him on the street, he would be the last person you would identify as having money. One such gentleman we met in our travels used to say to his pastor (especially in the winter), "Now Reverend, please call before you come to visit so I can turn the thermostat up from 55 to 60 degrees. I would not want you to be uncomfortable in my home."

"Old Clyde" Types
The Millionaire Next Door

It is interesting to note that this individual left million-dollar gifts to a college and his church. Now, I am not saying that the old Clyde-type person in your city may not leave your organization a nice chunk of change. But in today's world, it is more likely to happen to an organization that invested some time *romancing* this donor, loving him and caring about him for many years. Sure, there are exceptions to this rule, but they are becoming much more rare. Truly, it is all about romance, building and enhancing a relationship.

A few years ago, I won a Diet Coke in a very small side bet while conducting a strategic planning weekend with a new client. They had received a $5 million gift from a donor, so I encouraged them to invite him to their planning session. He was, after all, a stakeholder in the organization. A couple of the staff members said, "Okay, wise guy, let's see if you can identify this key donor." Bear in mind, I had only met a few of the people participating in this advancement/planning weekend. We had almost thirty staff, board, and volunteers participating. Virtually everyone showed up in nicely pressed khakis and Cutter & Buck golf shirts. All but one. He was dressed in navy blue Dickey work pants, a short-sleeve cowboy cut shirt, and a pair of funky looking tennis shoes that were not Nike's.

You must think of this relationship like you would a good marriage...

At the first break (and there were no nametags until after that break), I let the staff and planning team know who their major donor was. I won the Diet Coke easily. "How did you know?" they asked. "It was easy," I said. "Only one person at this event does not really care how he looks." This very wealthy donor was not attempting to set any kind of fashion statement. He was very comfortable and secure in his casual—and I mean *very* casual—attire. He did not care about how he looked or what people thought. He was not quite an "Old Clyde" type person, but he was close. Most major donors have a bit of a "my way" attitude about them. After all, they have made it and often have no need to attempt to impress anyone.

Love and Marriage: The Way of Love

What do we mean by "Romancing a Donor?" "Pat," I can hear you say, "how dare you compare love and marriage to something as trivial as fund-raising!?" On the contrary, I believe a marriage with your major donors has many parallels to good marriages in our society. Let me explain. While there are a number of definitions for *Romance*, here is a good one from the *Encarta Dictionary*: Romance is "[a characteristic of love], especially when the other person or relationship is idealized or exciting and intense." It could also be defined as a state of connectedness between people, (especially an emotional connection).

Two-word definitions read "to woo," "to court," "to solicit," "to chase," "to pursue," "to love." Think about how you can apply these definitions and the Romance process to your major donors. Romance is very much an educational process. You are getting to know about your date and you are helping your date to get to know you. Romance is by no means a one-way street. For it to truly work, clear communication is needed both ways. Romance is a sharing of values—yours and theirs. It is not just a right-brain, left-brain issue; *it is all about the heart*. If you want to get the support of major donors for projects now *and* in the future, you need to *win their hearts*.

How do you know you are in love? This question needs to be answered. What characteristics of love are you looking for in a relationship, and what characteristics are your major donors looking for from you and your organization? In his paraphrase translation, Eugene Peterson puts a unique spin on I Corinthians 13.

"If I speak with human eloquence and angelic ecstasy but don't love, I'm nothing but the creaking of a rusty gate. If I speak God's Word with power, revealing all His mysteries and making everything plain as day, and if I have faith that says to a mountain 'jump' and it jumps, but I don't have love, I'm nothing. If I give everything I own to the poor and even go to the stake to be burned as a martyr, but I don't have love, I've gotten nowhere. So no matter what I say, what I believe, and what I do, I'm bankrupt without love.

Love never gives up.
Love cares more for others than for self.
Love doesn't want what it doesn't have.
Love doesn't strut.
Doesn't have a swelled head.
Doesn't force itself on others.
Isn't always 'me first.'
Doesn't fly off the handle.
Doesn't keep score of the sins of others.
Doesn't revel when others grovel.
Takes pleasure in the flowering of truth.
Puts up with anything.
Trusts God always.
Always looks for the best.
Never looks back.
But keeps going to the end.

Love never dies. Inspired speech will be over some day; praying in tongues will end; understanding will reach its limit. We know only a portion of the truth, and what we say about God is always incomplete. But when the Complete arrives, our incomplete will be canceled.

But for the right now, until the completeness, we have three things to do to lead us toward that consummation: Trust steadily in God, Hope unswervingly, Love extravagantly. And the best of the three is love." (The Message)

Wow, what an outline for a great relationship with anyone, but especially a major donor! Essentially, nine characteristics of love are outlined in this passage. Ask yourself if you have or if you are ready to display these characteristics to your major donors.

Patience	Humility	Good temper
Kindness	Courtesy	Absence of evil
Generosity	Unselfishness	Sincerity

This could be an excellent checklist as you begin or enhance a relationship with a major donor.

Romance Questions and Answers

Think about a best or very good friend. What kinds of things do you know about him? You know his name, can spell it correctly, and you know the first name of his spouse and children. You even know the names of his grandchildren. You know his birthday and anniversary dates. You know his favorite restaurant, his favorite food, and his hobbies. You know what sports he follows, and whether he is a golfer or Cubs fan. During this dating process you begin to discover this kind of key information.

How do you gather this information about donor prospects? Begin by asking simple and natural questions as you spend time in their homes, their summer cottages, on the golf course, at ball games, or out on their boats.

It is not just a right-brain, left-brain issue; it is all about the heart.

These are not questions you asked or discovered in the Research phase. Many of the answers can only be provided by donors personally. All the scientific research in the world would not tell you their favorite fish to catch or their favorite NBA player. All this is learned as you begin to "date" and "romance" them. You are not walking in with a clipboard and five pages of questions; these questions and answers come up naturally as you spend time with them. I often ask clients we are helping with the major-donor process, "Do you have their cell phone numbers? Can you page them on their phones because they have shared their personal ID# with you? Have you been in their homes in the past year, or better yet, have they been in *your* home in the past year? How much time have you spent with them in the past twelve months?" Remember, TIME and LOVE are commodities that some major donors want you to invest in them personally.

Hot Buttons

Part of the Romance process is determining likes and dislikes. Back when you were dating, or now that you are dating, would you continue to frequent a restaurant your date despised? Probably not, or at least not for long. By now, after more than thirty years of marriage, I at least know what my wife, Jane, likes and dislikes. I know where she likes to dine, what kinds of clothes she likes, and I am well acquainted with her passion for golf. I often ask the question, "What are the hot buttons that really get your major/mega donor friends going?" What causes them to pound the table and get excited? A donor in Pennsylvania said, "I want this project to become a reality so badly it makes my teeth hurt." It was her way of expressing her passion or her hot button for this project. I then asked her how badly her teeth hurt, and we moved quickly from the Romance to the Request stage. The figure she shared with me was a number that, in fact, did appear to have her in a bit of pain!

Work hard in the Romance phase to clearly identify what hot buttons in your area of need really excite your donors. If you can identify and help expand the area of interest for your donors, their gifts will be larger and their longevity—the years they participate financially with your organization—will be extended. Helping a donor buy into your strategic ministry plan is imperative early on in your Romance plans.

Perhaps the term is a bit overworked, but major donors are truly "purpose-driven" people and donors. They want to make a difference with their dollars, and this will become apparent early on as you begin courting them. You will realize that most of them have no interest in helping you address the past (debt service), or even help you address the present (annual/operational) needs. Most of them have the desire to help you buy, ensure, and create the *future* of your organization. Their hot button is often giving bigger dollars that will have a bigger impact. They are going to give to their area of passion, so help them discover their hot buttons and match them with your area of need.

> *...major donors are truly "purpose-driven" people and donors.*

Test Your Vision

The Romance phase is a good time to test the quality of your vision with your major donors. If you take nothing else from this chapter, please take this with you: THE QUALITY OF YOUR MINISTRY VISION WILL IMPACT THE QUANTITY OF MAJOR/MEGA DONOR PARTICIPATION. Embed that concept *firmly* into your organizational strategy. If your vision is incomplete, or if your vision is unclear (or frankly, if it is unreasonable), you will not capture the heart, mind, soul, and checkbook of the major donor. Even if you push the right hot buttons (but cannot pull it off, or it just doesn't fit) you may lose the major-donor prospect early in the Romance phase.

"Without vision, people perish." Without vision, your organization will miss out on some of its greatest potential and eventually die. It is the major donors of this world who can help you realize the full potential of your organization. To run a test balloon of sorts with your clearly defined, on-paper, vision statement is a great Romance step. Ask your major/mega donors point blank, "Is our vision one that you understand, appreciate, and could help us implement?" It's a significant question that needs to be raised early on in the relational/Romance process. By testing your vision, you have the opportunity to tweak it, or at the very least help bring clarity to it.

On page 88 is a strategic planning outline many organizations we have worked with have used to help facilitate the Romance process. If you do not have a written strategic plan, this is a great outline to work with as you create the desired vision and future for your organization.

Here also is a list of cultivating tips to help you with the Romance process.

Thirty-One Ways to Cultivate Your Donors
By Stephen Hitchcock

1 Invite donors to visit.
2 Visit them.
3 Arrange meetings for them with other major donors.
4 Invite them to join your board.
5 Ask them to host major donor parties.
6 Ask them for advice.
7 Take them to funded projects.
8 Send them notes or cards on birthdays or anniversaries.
9 Send them flowers when in the hospital.
10 Send gifts with personal notes.
11 Send press clippings and notes when they are published or recognized in the news.
12 Send photos of those who benefit from their donation.
13 Give them handicrafts or artwork by beneficiaries of your programs.
14 Send certificates.
15 Write and call to thank them personally.
16 Install a dedicated 800-number to make it easy for them to contact you.
17 Invite them to join an honorary or advisory board.

18 Look for ways to develop shared interests.

19 Invite them to join delegations or go on trips.

20 Send them questionnaires.

21 Send them copies of your public service announcements (PSAs) and news releases.

22 Send videotapes about your agency's work.

23 Send your newsletter to them via first class mail in envelopes.

24 Issue press releases about major gifts.

25 Regularly ask them for more gifts.

26 Make every request a thank-you.

27 Send them copies of your direct mail packages, either preceded by a note of explanation and/or with cover notes.

28 Establish a memorial or tribute gifts program.

29 Host their son or daughter.

30 Hold special events or activities at the local or neighborhood level.

31 Establish a donor recognition program.

Key Elements of Strategic Planning

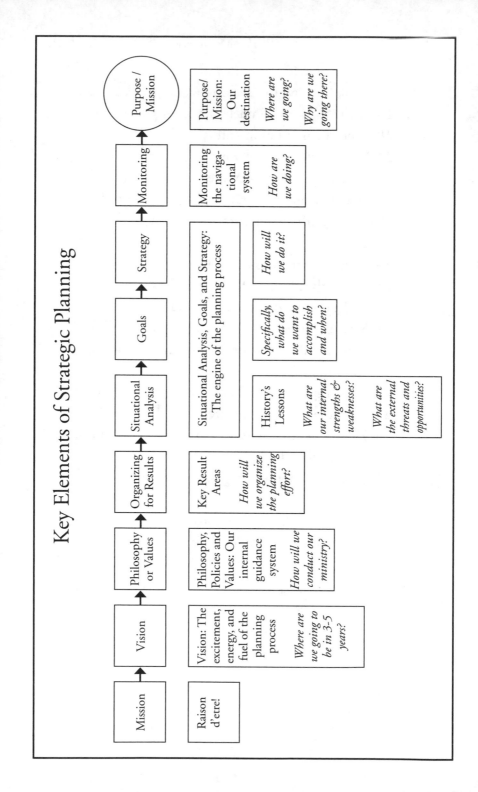

Mission	Vision	Philosophy or Values	Organizing for Results	Situational Analysis	Goals	Strategy	Monitoring	Purpose / Mission

Raison d'etre!

Vision: The excitement, energy, and fuel of the planning process

Where are we going to be in 3-5 years?

Philosophy, Policies and Values: Our internal guidance system

How will we conduct our ministry?

Key Result Areas

How will we organize the planning effort?

Situational Analysis, Goals, and Strategy: The engine of the planning process

History's Lessons

What are our internal strengths & weaknesses?

What are the external threats and opportunities?

Specifically what do we want to accomplish and when?

How will we do it?

Monitoring the navigational system

How are we doing?

Purpose/Mission: Our destination

Where are we going?

Why are we going there?

When Is the Romance Complete?

There are two answers to the question, "When is the Romance complete?" The first answer is never. Just like in a good marriage, the romance process is ongoing. The second answer is that the donor will usually tell you when it's time for the next step, the Request. All of us who are or have been married knew when it was time to ask for the commitment. But you will know, and your major/mega donor prospect will know.

On a first donor visit with a college president, the donor had some great questions. With his own two college students attending full-time and living in the dormitory, he asked why the college couldn't make it with his almost $50,000 annual tuition investment. The president took a yellow pad and sketched out the college budget. In a rough pie chart, he showed this major-donor prospect where the college allocated its resources. After the president had answered all of the donor's questions, the donor said, "How could I help you today?" Catch this, the Romance basically came to an end after a personal visit of about ninety minutes. The president stated, "My purpose in our visit today was to get to know you and share a broad perspective of our needs. Could I get back in touch with you in the next couple of weeks and bring you a personalized partnership proposal?" The donor said yes, and the deal was well on the way toward closure. Essentially, the Romance was complete; we were heading toward a Request.

Please do not shortchange yourself in this phase of your

major-donor strategy. You are moving the relationship forward and sometimes it takes more than one or two dates to get ready to make an ask/request. In the aforementioned story, while it was the first visit by the president, the donor was already a customer (not yet an investor) with two children attending this four-year institution. The president fairly quickly completed the Romance phase and prepped him for the Request. You will know when the time and the timing are right.

Find major donors who have a true love and passion for giving and help them discover how they can realize that true love and passion through your organization. If you do, like in the song "Some Enchanted Evening," you will never have to dream all alone. Romance is an important key to any great relationship. Work hard on making those enchanted relationships a reality.

Discover Your "Pat Answers" To These Thought-Provoking Questions

1. What has been your strategy to meet and greet major-donor prospects and suspects in the past?
2. Define what a Romance visit with you and your CEO might look like to a major/mega donor?
3. Should these Romance visits take place at your organization, in donors' homes, or some combination?

5

It's All about the Request

*Ask and it will be given to you; seek and
you will find; knock and the door will be
opened to you.*
—Matthew 7:7

It has been said that nothing really happens in life until something is sold. I'm not sure I completely buy into that. But I must admit that many donor calls just don't come to fruition because the Request is blown—either because it's never made at all or people are just unsure of what to do. Very little selling takes place *and there is little or no buy-in by the major donors*. If you have developed a major-donor relationship to the point of making a Request, why would you get cold feet? At one of the most important phases of the major-donor relationship, why would you suddenly become timid? Why, I ask, would you back up at this critical juncture? What happened between the great Romance visits and your preparation for the Request? Or perhaps even worse, you or those on your major-donor team begin making decisions for the major-donor prospect. "Oh, I am not really sure they would have an interest in making that kind of commitment." You put words in their mouths and begin speaking for them. Please, please, please avoid this at all costs!

Breaking through the Glass Ceiling

This concept of breaking through the glass ceiling is not new to anyone in the sales, relationship, or stewardship industry. Are you familiar with the concept? You or your organization are below the glass ceiling and your major/mega donor prospects are above the ceiling. You can see them, you know who they are. You even believe they are interested in your organization. Now comes the $64 thousand question, or perhaps (literally) the $6.4 million question, how do you break through to finally get a gift from them? How do you get through to really communicate your uniqueness, your mission, vision, and core values?

If you have worked through your Research and Romance phases, you are ready to break through. The Request will solidify the relationship. While you may not get the gift you desired on the first Request, you will have broken through the ceiling. I believe the Request and the gift

92

begin to confirm that the ceiling has been broken, that now you are at least within reach of these individuals. You have Researched their interest, and educated and tested their passion through your Romance phase. Now comes the Request. It must be done in a "Golden Rule" (how would you want to be treated in a similar situation) fashion. If those rules of relationship are honored, the ceiling is broken and "buy in" is achieved through the Request.

The "S" Word

After almost a thousand major-donor presentations, I am convinced that *solicitation* is not a dirty word. We solicit each other virtually every day of our lives. "Excuse me, could you tell me what time it is?" "Pardon me, but have you ever eaten at the BBQ place down on 6th Avenue? Is it any good?" "Hey, Kate (one of my crew members), can you help me with my laptop? It's acting weird again." "Do you know where Sutherland Street is?" You get the idea, we all solicit each other on a regular basis. Many major donors have shared with us that they want and *expect* to be asked. If done properly, appropriately, and tastefully, this is one more positive step in your major-donor program. Personally, based on my years of experience, I think this stage is the most fun of the multi-phased major-donor process. Yes, you heard correctly, asking people to make a major investment in moving your organization forward is *fun*.

Are you aware of the close ratios here in America, Canada, and the U.K.? What is the *most frequently* used funding method in America? Direct mail, or what is often defined as written communication. What is the *least* used method of solicitation in America? Personal solicitation, or what is often defined as one-on-one, kneecap-to-kneecap communication. It's up front and it's personal! What is the *least effective* solicitation/fund-raising method used in America? Direct mail/written communication, with a 1-5 percent close ratio across the board!

> *I am convinced that* solicitation *is not a dirty word.*

In other words, if you send out one hundred letters and get five responses you fall within national norms of gift expectancy. One dear lady in Minneapolis, Donna Stelmaszewski, kept track of the number of direct mail fund-raising pieces she received over a twelve-month period—1,430! The article in the *Metro Star Tribune* indicated she gave to very few of the organizations, but she got lots of mail. Even the most discerning donor would have trouble deciding where to give.

I know what you are thinking. You will be quick to say, "Hey, Pat, we do not send out too much mail and we average an 11 percent response rate to our direct mail letters." That's great! Congratulations, you are well above the national norms. Do you know what the *most effective* form of solicitation is in America? Personal solicitation, one-on-one personal contact. Our experience indicates a 75-80 percent close ratio—and often for the amount requested in the solicitation document!

Here are the average fund-raising close ratios we've

experienced from the fifteen hundred clients we've served over the past couple of decades.

Methodology	Close Ratio
Direct Mail	1-5%
Telephone	30% (often with lapsed donors)
Group Events	50%, if they know it is a fund-raising event, and if the right person invites them to attend (friend-raising factor).
Personal Solicitation	75-80%+, again if the right person makes the request and the prospective donor has a relationship with your organization, or is a key player (board, staff, faculty, volunteer, CEO, etc.).

If direct mail is the least effective and personal solicitation is the most effective, why do we have it upside down in our fund-raising practices in America? Think about it, one major/mega-donor visit could produce more gift income next year than one, two, or even three direct mail drops (DMK—direct mail kit)! Yet many organizations refuse to visit their major-donor prospects and suspects. "It is too expensive." "I would not know what to say." "They tell me they are too busy; I should just send them a letter." "Our CEO is a lousy fund-raiser; in fact he/she indicated there had been no personal call to do that here at our organization." Why are we afraid to build relationships with our major-donor prospects and suspects? This is not rocket science, it is in fact all about relationships! We have to overcome our fear, in some ways a fear of the *unknown*.

The FUD Factor

This is all-important. Many major-donor relationships are never consummated because of FUD: Fear, Uncertainty, and Doubt. We the solicitors suffer from the FUD syndrome, not the major donor. Overcoming this FUD obstacle will absolutely change your advancement office mentality, production, performance, and net gift income. Your capital campaigns will get funded. You will begin to lay a foundation for endowment funding. Overcoming the FUD syndrome will make an impact.

Fear grips all of us at different times in our lives. You know that nail-biting, worry-about-all-kinds-of-things fear. In most major-donor relationships, we fear the loss of the relationship. We have carefully Researched and Romanced this particular donor and now we are afraid of making "the

Fear, uncertainty, and doubt are killers to any major-donor program.

ask," or making it in the wrong way, so fear takes over. "Oh my, what if we ask too high and we offend them? After all, a damaged relationship is very difficult to restore. We have worked this hard to get them to this point with our organization, so perhaps we had better wait. We certainly do not want to offend them." Perhaps they will even approach us and indicate somewhat out of the clear blue sky what they might be willing to invest. Remember a concept mentioned earlier: No heavenly hinting.

Most of all, we fear rejection. We fear the pain of hearing a NO! Sometimes we even fear hearing a NOT RIGHT NOW! We are uncertain how to craft material to take along on the call, or how to conduct a brief Request session. We begin to feed our fear, uncertainty, and doubt with state-

The FUD Factor

ments like, "I doubt if they (the potential major donors) would have any interest in helping to fund this project." Fear, uncertainty, and doubt are killers to any major-donor program. You *must* begin to address and eliminate the FUD factor in your organization. Sit down as a fund-raising team, an advancement team, with your trustee board, development team, or campaign committee and honestly evaluate the FUD factor that has limited your success to date. As you begin to honestly address the fear, uncertainty, and doubt, you are one more step closer to having an effective major-donor program.

Be Specific

There are a variety of schools of thought on the issue of being specific. "Be very specific" is what I have learned time and time again. Make the Request specific. What do you want them to consider, when do you want them to make the gift, and how else can they help with the project? If we have all been blessed with measures of time, talent, and treasure, is the relationship strong enough to ask for all three? A great question only you and your major-donor team can answer, but one you need to address.

Practically speaking, would you invite someone to take a job in your company and not be specific? "Pat, would you consider working for our firm?" "Yes!" I reply. "But what would you like me to do for your company?" "Oh, just fit in anywhere, kind of do whatever you like." Does that sound a bit far-fetched? Or how about this? You are putting together a baseball team and you begin to recruit players. You are the coach, yet you say to the team at game time, "Hey, just play wherever you like today. Where, really doesn't matter." This would be total chaos and even thinking about winning the game would be unrealistic.

Yet, when it comes to being specific about the role we need our major donors to fulfill, we do the same thing. We are afraid to ask. Many organizations get "tipped" with the 3 T's (time, talent & treasure) of the major donor because they are fearful of being specific. "Oh, let's just let them decide." Certainly people who have major/mega donor capacity are decisive people, but in most cases you will not offend them with a specific request. Yes, I do mean a specific dollar request and the invitation for them to invest time as a fund-raiser or as a friend-raiser. After all, most major donors know and spend quality time with other major donors.

Donor Rating Session

Prior to making a Request, a rating session should take place. A small group of people from your major-donor team needs to schedule a session to put a dollar figure together for each of your major-donor prospects. Do I have a formula for this? Is someone going to give you some hidden secret to help you decide on a number? The answer, again, is yes and no.

Let's take no first. We have already discussed how there is both art and science to all that we do in the donor field.

I believe in addition to your Research and Romance you need to be "artsy," or perhaps a bit "gut level," in determining a gift range. There is not a magic formula based upon their income and perceived ability (remember the best-selling book *The Millionaire Next Door*), it's just what you *hope* they might consider. Obviously, you cannot be crazy or way off the mark, but an aggressive ask normally will not offend a donor. We have been asked many times how we determined the number or the range of giving requested. Simply state the facts: "Our major-donor team held a rating session and (fill in the blank) was suggested by our team." Remember to use the Golden Rule. How would you like to be treated in a similar situation? Keep this foremost in your thinking, even in the rating process. Be fair, or as I like to say, be "graciously aggressive."

Now let's look at the yes. Here is a formula that is a bit more scientific. You have done quality research and have discovered their area of interest. You have done some form of "hard asset" research. You have some idea of their net worth and giving patterns to other charitable projects. You have really honed in on their area of interest and passion, and they have even indicated that, if they are really excited about a project, they might consider giving 50 percent of the need. With that information you have a formula to proceed. Ask questions, create scenarios, and share specific time lines. "If we can raise this much, by this date, we can break ground and have the foundation and building going up in the spring. Or, with 50 percent in cash and commitments, we can employ the new technology faculty, and open the new science and technology center, *and* be ready for students by next fall." Yes, the process we have and will continue to recommend, will help you be *very specific* with an amount or range of giving for your major/mega donors.

In a visit with a mega donor and his wife for another organization, we had been specific about a request they had granted. In the course of conversation, he mentioned their favorite Christian college was in the leadership/ quiet phase of a major capi-tal campaign. He did not directly share the size of their gift, but he indicated

Ask questions, create scenarios, and share specific time lines.

the campaign goal was $25 million, and that they had already indicated their pledge to give one half of the campaign goal. This humble major donor never mentioned a dollar figure, he let us do the math. They were excited and very specific about the size and shape of their gift early in this campaign. Do you have the feeling there was some immediate campaign momentum and excitement? Me too! More than likely, in the feasibility/pre-campaign study, dollar figures were discussed with the couple (she served on the board). Early in the leadership phase, in a rating and asking process, their gift was secured. These folks were excited about the vision of the college and pleased to be part of turning this goal into a reality.

Setting the Appointment

In today's busy world, many major-donor asks go south because the appointment is never made. Time is often bartered now like money was a few generations ago. In fact, some people make the statement, "I have more money than I have time." So a critical step in the major-donor process gets missed if you do not make the appointment. Note: IT IS IMPORTANT THAT YOU DO NOT ASK FOR THE GIFT DURING THE TELEPHONE CONTACT. YOUR ONLY PURPOSE FOR THE CALL IS TO SET THE APPOINTMENT. Please take this critical note away with you! It is so easy to give in when resistance starts to rise, but hold your ground and set an appointment to meet them live and in person.

Consider this phone scenario. The major-donor prospect says, "Hey, we know your organization, we are going to give, just send me the information (the proposal)." Maybe this sounds familiar, and to others it even sounds good! Why *not* send it to them by mail or email? Remember our close ratio perspective mentioned earlier in the chapter? When you mail a major-donor proposal, in my humble opinion, it just becomes an upgraded piece of direct mail. Direct mail has a 1-5 percent close ratio. Personal contact has a 75-80+ percent close ratio. Are you willing to work hard and build the relationship through careful Research and Romance, and then allow the Request to become another piece of direct mail?

I hope your answer is NO! Yes, they are busy people,

and you are busy as well. But with patience, persistence, and flexibility, you can set an appointment. A personal appointment to meet with a couple in their home and share the request is *by far* the most productive route. Let them know you will need about thirty minutes to share your case/leadership proposal. No need to spend the entire evening. In fact, they will appreciate your prompt response and to-the-point sharing. If they ask you to stay longer, that's their decision, but you have honored your thirty-minute agreement. Be firm but fair in setting the appointment, but please do not mail a proposal you worked so hard to develop.

Here is another potential scenario. "Bill, this is Pat from the college (or mission or whatever). In our last discussion, you indicated you would welcome a partnership proposal from our organization. (I'm assuming good Romance has already taken place). Would Tuesday evening work for you and Betty to meet for thirty minutes to allow me to share this proposal in person? Or how about Thursday, would that work better? Yes, I could make it at 8:30 on Saturday morning."

Or it might go like this, "Yes, Bill, I could be at your office at 2:30 on Wednesday. Could Betty join us for thirty minutes to discuss this opportunity to invest in the future of our ministry?"

Set a personal appointment. Your best work will be accomplished face to face in their home or office to present your proposal in person. I can share a multitude of stories about how a successful Request probably would never have happened if we had mailed the proposal or the Request document instead of making a personal visit. With the added personal touch, you can read the donor, the donor can read you, and you can both ask questions. It is such an important step that too often, believe it or not, gets missed or at least misdirected.

Anatomy of the Visit

I have a daughter-in-law in medical school at Emory University in Atlanta. She is preparing to become a physician assistant. Her father is an orthopedic surgeon and her grandfather is an OB-GYN. This is a family that knows anatomy.

When it comes to a donor visit, it is all about knowledge and fit. You will get better at both as you make calls and continue to make personal solicitation visits. The fit part is working totally with their schedule. You need to make it fit

When it comes to a donor visit, it is all about knowledge and fit.

their schedule, not the other way around. If a major donor wants to meet at 10:00 a.m. or 10:00 p.m., you need to be willing to re-schedule your visit around their time and willingness to meet. Too many CEOs, executive directors, presidents, and advancement officers seem to want the major donor to bend and flex to fit their schedule. If the relationship is really strong, that might fit. But if it is not, you need to make it work on their time table.

When you enter their house, they will want to seat you in a living area with a couple of love seats or a sofa and some chairs. Politely ask if you can sit at the kitchen or dining room table. Why? What if you want to share a brief CD/DVD presentation on your laptop? The kitchen table is great. If you have a personalized proposal with you, even with keen eyesight, it is impossible for them to see from the other love seat across the room. You will constantly be moving toward them, back to your love seat, then toward them, and back to your seat. Your presentation will be much more natural if you sit at the table. It also makes serving coffee or tea much more safe and simple. (A cup of coffee spilled on white plush carpeting is not only a mess but totally disrupts the visit.) It also helps you stick with your thirty-minute time limit for the presentation of the Request. My best work with major/mega donors over the years, whether it is Research (feasibility study/pre-campaign study research) or Request (presenting an ask in a brief meeting), has been at a kitchen, dining room, or board room table. Even if you are in the office of the executive, there is often a 42" round table with four chairs away from the desk. You want the atmosphere to be relaxed yet business like, and often the desk in their office is not as good as the small table.

Many years ago someone mentioned to me the importance of the 3 B's in any donor visit. Unless it is an extended Research or Romance call, or they have invited you to stay on past your agreed-upon time frame, the 3 B's are a pretty safe plan. Be Good, Be Brief, and Be Gone. Ponder that for a few seconds. If you think about it, there is great wisdom in this simple concept! Remember, no heavenly hinting. You can be direct, and in doing so be somewhat brief. It does not take three hours to make a major/mega donor ask! The Request can be all of these three B's. Then the donors might invite you to stay to view a video of their family, play pool in the family room, or carefully drink coffee in the parlor over the white plush carpet and talk politics, religion, or both. But remember, the Request portion of your meeting is *over*. Now you are back to additional Romance activities and perhaps beginning to jump ahead to the next R, Recruitment. My point is that you are now on their time and *they* have invited you to stay, so you are very safe in doing so. (But don't spill your coffee, unless you know a really good carpet cleaning company.)

Be Good, Be Brief, and Be Gone.

Simple Tips from a Couple of Simple Men

Will Rogers was a modern-day Mark Twain and had the capacity to share very simple yet profound truths. Will is quoted as saying "The common thing about common sense is it ain't that common." This is a simple yet so profound "Golden Rule" statement. Use common sense in making a Request of any donor, but especially those who have significant capacity. If you were a high-capacity donor, how would you want to be asked for a gift? Use the Golden Rule. Use common sense and ask those questions well in advance of your solicitation/Request visit.

A second, longer quote is from John David Rockefeller Jr. in a speech he gave to a group of solicitors preparing for a large campaign, titled "The Technique of Soliciting Funds." It is so profound yet so simple that I want to quote a major section for you. It reads a bit rough because it is a transcribed speech he gave to charge up the fund-raising troops. The speech was made in the 60's and it is a bit male-centric. But nowhere have I found a better, more simple, common-sense, Golden Rule approach to giving. And I do believe Mr. Rockefeller knew what he was talking about. Do you think he had a few pitches made to him throughout his life?

"I have been asked to say a few words on the technique of soliciting donations.

"Perhaps the best way to acquire a knowledge of that subject is to ask ourselves the question 'How would I like to be approached for a gift?' The answer, if carefully thought out, may be relied upon as a pretty safe guide to the task of soliciting. I have been brought up to believe and the conviction only grows on me, that giving ought to be entered into in just the same careful way as investing—that giving is investing and that it should be tested by the same intelligent standards. Whether we expect dividends in dollars or in human betterment, we need to be sure that the gift or the investment is a wise one and therefore we should know all about it. By the same token, if we are going to solicit other people to interest them in giving to a particular enterprise we must be able to give them adequate information in regard to it, such information as we would want were we considering a gift.

"First of all, then a solicitor must be well informed in regards to the salient facts about the enterprise for which he is soliciting. Just what is its significance, its importance? How sound is the organization back of it, how well organized? How great is the need? An accurate knowledge of these and similar facts is necessary in order that the solicitor may be able to speak with conviction.

"It is a great help to know something about the person whom you are approaching. You cannot deal successfully with all people the same way. Therefore, it is desirable to find out something about the person you are going to visit—what his interest[s] are, whether you have any friends in common, whether he gave last year, if so how much he gave, what he might be able to give this year, etc. Information such as that put[s] you more closely in touch with him and make[s] the approach easier.

"Again one always likes to know what other people are giving. That may be an irrelevant question, but it is a human question. If I am asked for a contribution, naturally and properly I am influenced in deciding how much I should give by what others are doing.

"Another suggestion I like to have made [to] me by a solicitor is how much it is hoped I will give. Of course such a suggestion can be made in a way that might be most annoying. I do not like to have anyone tell me what it is my duty to give. There is just one [man] who is going to decide that question—who has the responsibility of deciding it—and [he] is myself. But I do like a man to say to me, 'John we are trying to raise $5,000,000 and hoping you might be desirous of giving $500,000. If you see your way clear to do so, it will be an enormous help and encouragement. You may have it in mind to give more; if so we shall be glad. On the other hand, you may feel you cannot give as much, in view of other responsibilities. If that is the case, we shall understand. Whatever you give after thinking the matter over carefully in light of the need, your other obligations and your desire to do your full share as a citizen [will] be gratefully received and deeply appreciated.' When you talk like that to a man, he is glad to meet you again and will not take the other elevator when he sees you in the corridor because you backed him to the wall and forced him to give.

"Of supreme importance is to make a pleasant, friendly contact with the prospective giver. Some people have a less keen sense of their duty and responsibility with others. With them, a little urging may be helpful. But with most people a convincing presentation of the facts and the need is far more effective. When a solicitor come[s] to you and lays on your heart the responsibility that rests so heavily on his; when his earnestness gives convincing evidence of how seriously interested he is; when he makes it clear that he knows you are no less anxious to do your duty in the manner [than]he is, that you are just as conscientious, that he feels sure all you need is to realize the importance of the enterprise and the urgency of the need in order to lead you to do your full share in meeting it—he has made you his friend and brought you to think of giving as a privilege.

"Never think you need to apologize for asking someone to give to a worthy object, any more than as though you were giving him an opportunity to participate in a high grade investment. The duty of giving is as much his as is the duty of asking yours. Whether or not he should give to that particular enterprise, and if so how much is for him alone to decide.

"To recapitulate then, briefly, know your subject; be so sold on it yourself that you can convincingly present its claims in the fewest possible words. A letter may well precede an interview but personal contact is the most effective. Know as much as you can about the man to whom you go; give him a general idea to the contributions being made by others in his group, and suggest in a gracious and tactful way what you would be glad to have him give, leaving it entirely to him to decide what he shall give.

"Be kindly and considerate. Thus you will get closest to a [man's] heart and his pocketbook."

WOW, is that a great stewardship speech! It covers many of the topics we have already shared and some that are still on the way. Simple yet profound is the only way to go forward with your major-donor prospects and suspects.

The Elevator Pitch

What if John David Rockefeller Jr. invited you to ride to the top of the Empire State Building in New York City? The express elevator is a sixty-second ride. JDR asks this question, "So, Pat, tell me about your organization and what you are doing in the world to make it a better place?" You have sixty seconds to give the pitch. What do you say? Here is an outline to help you with your sixty-second presentation. I am convinced if you can tell your story in sixty seconds, and if you have thirty to forty minutes to make an ask, you will be awesome. Have some fun and fill in the blanks of the sixty-second pitch.

THE 60-SECOND PITCH

HISTORY
MISSION
IMPORTANCE (of your existence)
THE NEED
YOUR PROGRAM (address the need)
THE COST ($ & ¢)
THE ASK ($)
THE CLOSE

Ergonomics

Ergonomics is a Detroit design term that has everything to do with the fit. Your 2007 Pontiac fits you better than my dad's '58 Pontiac Bonneville, which he bought new that year. The seats of your 2007 model are wider in the bottom, the mirrors are more user-friendly, and the vision is much improved. Ergonomics is the ongoing study of the fit.

Make sure your Request fits you and fits the needs of the major/mega donor. Treat every major donor as a mini-campaign. Personalize the Request proposal to fit their needs, their timing, and their investment opportunities, always reminding them that their investment in your organization is an eternal investment.

Most of all, as an organization, you need to be comfortable with the ask, with the Request. It cannot be forced and it needs to be a common-sense approach to your need for resources and their need to help meet those human needs.

Never think you need to apologize for asking someone to give to a worthy object...
—J.D. Rockefeller Jr.

Discover Your "Pat Answers"
To These Thought-Provoking Questions

1. Can you list or name a couple of glass ceilings you need to break through?
2. Is the word *solicitation* a naughty word in your organization?
3. Is FUD a reality in your organization as it relates to personal contact with major donors?
4. Have you ever done any major-donor rating? If not, why not?
5. Do you often or never ask your high-capacity donors for a specific amount?
6. How many donors do you think you could visit personally in the next month/year?
7. Can you identify the first three of the 5 R's (Research, Romance, and Request) in the Rockefeller speech?

6

It's All about Recognition

He who gives early gives twice.
—Miguel de Cervantes

Say thanks and really, really mean it!

Saying thanks *and meaning it* is critical to a successful major/mega donor program. We have become very good at asking for money, but sometimes we are not as well versed at saying thanks. A very simple thank you is all it takes to bring closure to the first three phases in the major/mega donor process.

So Recognize your major donors. Just discover an appropriate way to thank them and encourage them to stay connected with your organization. Obviously, if it is a multi-year gift, you have opportunity for multiple thank-you touches. If it is a one-time gift you must be prepared to thank them and begin to build the platform for the next gift. Not to be crass—you are not saying thank you to get another gift. But you are continuing to foster that major-donor environment at your organization.

Penny-Wise but Pound-Foolish

I was on the faculty of Stewardship Services (the Christian Stewardship Association of the U.K.) in their first conference on "giving" in Coventry, England, in 2003. The event was attended by just over one hundred charity leaders, pastors, and denominational stewardship officers, there to garner a better understanding of giving in the U.K. We had about eighty people from England, Ireland, Scotland, and Wales. It was a fun event, and they soaked up the biblical perspective on stewardship. We also determined that, even though there are a few minor cultural differences, many of the methods employed in America have been successful in the U.K.

Treat every major donor as a mini-campaign.

While walking them through the principles in this book, we got to the whole issue of Recognition, and a very interesting question was raised. A vicar from the Church of England (I think he would be an assistant pastor here in America) had the following question: "Pat, in regard to this issue, I have a parishioner who gave a 10,000 pound gift eighteen months ago to a ministry organization in this room, and he or she still does not have a receipt or a thank-you note. Is that appropriate?" By now you have read and absorbed enough of my perspective to answer that question just as I did. If giving is all about relationships, then this relationship had been injured, broken, or perhaps both. The obvious question is, why the delay and what should be done to begin to restore that relationship? We discussed it as a group, and in true American style, I encouraged all of them to say thank you early and often in the donor process. Truly, that organization was on the verge of being penny-wise but pound-foolish. Take really good care of your major donors and spend a dollar or two saying thanks. It will pay great dividends in the long run. After all, the gift for which you are saying thank you is probably not the final gift from that major-donor. As the relationship grows and blossoms, so will the opportunity to share additional needs and grow the partnership.

How Much Is Too Much?

My friend Jim Schottman was an advancement officer for a large medical facility connected to a university. In the mid 80's, Jim did some consulting work with me, and one day we were discussing saying thanks and meaning it. He blew me away by saying, "For a significant gift to the hospital we say thanks seven times." Wow, as previously mentioned, some organizations have trouble saying thanks even once. How do you do it seven times?

For a gift of $10,000 or more, they said thanks seven times, and here's how it worked:

- The donor got two thank-you notes or telephone calls from people who had been recipients of care in the cardiac unit in the past 90-120 days.
- The donor received two thank-you notes from cardiologists who worked within that department, thanking the donor for making it possible for them to continue to perform amazing surgeries on the heart.
- The president of the university hospital sent a thank-you note or made a phone call.
- The head of Cardiology sent a thank-you note on behalf of the entire staff.
- The development/advancement officer assigned to that person sent a thank-you note.

Yes, that composed the seven thank-you touches. Is that too much? Is it overkill, and does it cause the donor to say, "Hey, enough already"? Jim and his team seemed to get a whole lot more positive indications than negative indications in this process. By the way, most of the notes were handwritten. I know our laser printers make beautiful script, bold upper and lower case letters, and will even underline, but that is not nearly as effective as a heart-felt, handwritten thank-you note.

A Cell-Phone Relationship

As we all know by now, a cell-phone revolution is underway around the world. China has more cell phones than the United States has people! I am convinced you need to get the cell phone numbers of your key donors. Why would you need their cell phone numbers? It is a very personal way to contact them and acknowledge a gift by thanking them personally.

Case in point, this cell-phone revolution has impacted the way political campaigns are being conducted here in America. Many households in the U.S.A., Canada, and the U.K. no longer have a land line, they have gone totally cellular. Gone are the days an agency can purchase, beg, borrow, or steal your home telephone number. Pew Research Center recently reported that as many as 7.4% percent of the households in America do not have a home telephone number. You reach them by cell or not at all. This trend is only going to continue to escalate.

How many major-donor prospect cell phone numbers do you have? Some may send you a significant check and you'll be unable to call them and say thanks. They have no home number and you have no cell phone number for them. You are left to a high-tech (email) but not a high-touch method of Recognition. A handwritten note (a form of direct mail) is a great way to communicate, but what if they are traveling? What if it gets lost in the mail (imagine our postal service doing something like that) or it is stolen or destroyed in a postal sorting machine? Hey, it happens. To ensure that you can say thanks effectively, begin developing a cell phone list for all of your major donors. Understand, though, you will not get a cell phone number unless you have developed a relationship. Money may be easier

I am convinced you need to get the cell phone numbers of your key donors. to secure than the cell phone number! Obviously, do not misuse the cell-phone relationship. Use it for just the right occasion to say thank you, update the donor on specific information regarding your organization, or perhaps an invitation to play golf or attend a concert. Be smart and use it wisely.

One Time or a Lifetime

Think about your family. That is a lifetime relationship. Develop the same thought process with your major donors. If you grab the money and run, it will very likely be your last gift. The pattern of giving will continue to increase if your Recognition program is effective. Too many organizations only focus on the here and now, they are not looking forward. If you do not nurture the relationship, another organization may expand the relationship with that major donor.

Once again, ergonomics is a good test. Is your method of saying thanks consistent with your organization? Will it in some way offend the donor by being too opulent? Make sure your life-time Recognition plan fits your organization and your major donors.

Eternal Value

If you believe the work of your organization has eternal value, share that in your Recognition process. Let donors know the importance of their gifts now and let them know their investment is also long-term. Share with them how their gifts both impact their world and people in that world and have eternal value. This is such a great perspective that is often overlooked.

Please do not overlook or cut corners on your Recognition program. If you do it will impact the long-term, life-time relationship that is so important to you and your donors. Sit down as an organization and lay out a strategy for saying thanks. It may be simple or it may be complex, but you need to do a great job of caring for your donors.

Discover Your "Pat Answers" To These Thought-Provoking Questions

1. How quickly does your organization turn around a receipt and thank-you letter?
2. Do you have a pre-determined strategy for saying thank you to high-capacity donors?
3. What has been your most unique way of thanking a key donor?
4. Have you been guilty of "grabbing the money and running?"
5. What would be a unique way of saying thanks that would cost little or nothing but your time and creativity?

7

It's All about Recruitment

Inspire the best people to become your
best advocates.
—Unknown

Remember the donor comment I mentioned earlier that says, "I have more money than I have time." Many major/mega donors we have visited over the years have indicated a willingness to give money, but an investment of time is a much more difficult commodity. For you to be successful in the major-donor arena, however, you need your major donors to assist you in this process, and that will mean giving *their* time! You want and need to recruit them to assist you by becoming a "friend-raiser" and, where possible, a "fund-raiser" as well.

As a part-time umpire, I am struck by the fact that winning teams usually have great chemistry, and losing teams often have "issues." Baseball teams, like other sports franchises, win if they have good players. You have the opportunity to build a major-donor Recruitment team that will help you open doors for new donor relationships. It is an intentional process. People usually do not respond, "Wow, that process of sharing a major/mega gift has encouraged me to share the experience with all of my friends." They need you to help lead them to that action in the major-donor Recruitment strategy. (Are we trying to say recruit winners?)

I am convinced the ultimate test of major-donor relationships is this: Will they help you by opening doors of opportunity? Has your Research, your Romance strategy, an appropriate Request, and a very heartfelt Recognition opened the way to now Recruit your major donor to invest their time and relationships? Yes, you want them to help you by leading you to meet and engage their circle of influence. As you become effective with this fifth R in the donor cycle, you will remain busy and productive as a major/mega donor officer/representative. You will never run out of contacts as every major donor becomes a center of influence for entirely new major-donor relationships.

Major-Donor Acquisition

Every donor base has a funnel with two ends, the top and the bottom. You must continue to put new names in the top of the funnel as each year you lose donors out the bottom of the funnel. It's just a reality. People die, they retire and move to another city, they lose interest, and they even get mad. Let's be honest, we would all like to extend the life of our donor relationships, especially with our major donors. But we need to constantly stay in the acquisition business. New names, new relationships, new opportunities, and new money are the life

Your close ratio is very high when a major donor agrees to lead you to see a friend.

blood of any healthy organization. I believe virtually every organization is either growing and moving forward or is in decline and moving backward. There is no neutral gear for your organization. It is only "D" for drive or "R" for reverse. You must continue to acquire new donors or organizational atrophy will set in. I've seen it happen far too often with the clients we have helped.

Direct mail and some of the other fund-raising methods are all about cranking enough numbers. With major/mega donor acquisition, it is *all about relationships*. It's the right people leading you to see the people they know and paving the way for a new relationship. They do this by saying, "I know, love, and trust you and your organization, and because of that I am willing to put in a good word for you with my key contacts." Your close ratio is very high when a major donor agrees to lead you to see a friend. It almost always turns out to be a new donor relationship and often can become a major-donor relationship.

125

Donors communicate with their friends in a number of ways. Mail, telephone, email, an invitation to a small group event, and meeting them in person are the most obvious. The key to any communication is also pretty obvious. The more personal and intimate the contact the more opportunity for your current major donors to connect a major-donor friend to your organization.

Let me break down these communication methods and share some practical experience from the past twenty-five years.

1. **Personalized Mail**—I listen to my colleagues talk about major-donor packages. They are, more or less, an upgraded DMK (direct mail kit). They may be effective with a handful of major-donor prospects and suspects, but it is not going to work with the same impact as the 5 R's. By now I know you realize a personal visit is the most effective way to make a Request and to invite your major donor to begin thinking through the networking process. It is very difficult to ask a major donor to help you to "friend-raise" with a direct mail kit. Mail, however, may be a good way for major donors to share your ministry with one or more of their close friends. The opportunity to invite your major-donor friends to help you open doors with their friends will be more effective if done in a more personal way. A mailed request can work, if it is personalized for the major donor's use. Personalized letters, classy invitations, and clever email invitations are ways to in-

vite other major donor prospects to attend an event or schedule a personal visit. And a handwritten note still is a very effective way to communicate with a friend. But allow me to remind you again that we need to be high-touch in our high-tech world. So you see, mail can be used strategically, but it is limiting.

2. **Telephone Contact**—More personal than mail, the telephone can be a great tool to help recruit a major donor to attend an event or schedule a personal visit. As mentioned earlier, the cell phone has changed the way we do business in America. And the true test of a major-donor relationship is whether you have a cell phone number. On numerous occasions, I have been in the office of a major donor when they have said, "Please allow me to share a couple of other numbers where you can easily reach me." One major donor even gave me the direct office number, a vacation property number, a home number, and a cell phone number! Again, ask yourself with whom you have shared those numbers in your personal life. That's right, your very close friends! Please be very careful and wise, do not misuse any of these numbers from your key friends. The calls to major donors using these numbers are only to update, encourage, inform, and recruit. If you exploit your donor, the relationship will be brief.

   Encourage them by phone to attend an important major-donor briefing event. You might ask them to speak, pray, or just be present to add credibility to your event. Cell phones are often on 24/7, so know the time zone you are calling. As I write this book, we have clients in the U.K. with a five-hour time difference ahead of us and in Alaska with a four-hour time difference behind us. If I need to call a major donor in the U.K. to inquire about a donor briefing for Moorlands College, I need to factor in a nine-hour time difference. A cheery American telephone call at 2:00 a.m. U.K. time would neither be appreciated nor effective.

I am convinced that small group events are a great major-donor Recruitment strategy.

Summing this up, the telephone can be an effective tool in your arsenal of building and enhancing relationships with your major donors. A telephone call adds warmth and the personal touch that an email or a direct mail package just cannot provide. You will need that warmth and extra personal touch as you invite/recruit your major donors to help you with other key contacts. You will do so much better in the Recruitment process using the telephone.

3. **Small Group Events**—After years of trial and error (a good bevy of both!), I am convinced that small group events are a great major-donor Recruitment strategy. It is very unlikely that your largest and perhaps most mature major/mega donor prospects will come to a large dinner at a local hotel, hall, or at your location. While

sit-down dinner/banquets can be very effective if you plan and implement them correctly, a donor couple is much more likely to attend a small and intimate group event. Often this group event is held at a home, country club, or some unique, intimate setting. It is not about numbers. It is not a quantity issue, it's a quality issue. Getting the right people out to hear about your organization is what you want. It is about being invited by friends to their home to consider a project in which their good friends are already invested. Again, in this Recruitment phase, relationships are golden!

A Case Study for a Major-Donor Event That Really Worked

Many years ago, I was employed to help a struggling college attempt to put the wheels back on their advancement department. The president of the college had been asked to resign. He had led an effort to close the institution, and his resignation had been announced early in the spring term. You can just imagine what that did for fall enrollment! The college also had sold significant portions of the campus to developers and a large new-age church. They had cannibalized their assets from over fifty acres to under twenty acres. And you thought your organization had a few struggles!

Two vital issues were at stake with these decisions and the circumstances that resulted—bodies and bucks. Paying students (tuition) and donors (gift income) were unsure of the direction of the college. Students were choosing to go elsewhere, and donors were looking to give elsewhere, definitely not to this sinking ship. In very late spring/early summer, under new board leadership and after the return of a former president, the college decided to keep the institution open for the next fall. I was asked to begin re-building the advancement team starting July 1. A long-time VP of the institution described the environment this way: "Pat, we have lost half of our student body. If all goes well, we should only lose $1-$1.5 million in the operational fund this year. Oh, by the way, we think we have a pretty major PR problem." So I had very few students, even fewer dollars, and a major public relations challenge.

After much prayer, I accepted the contract and immediately began to do triage. I had to attempt to stop the bleeding somehow! All 4 R's (not the 5 R's) under my advancement leadership were in trouble. CR-Constituent Relationships were angry about the years of bad decisions. PR-Public Relations…the college image was in the tank and the local newspapers were having a field day watching board members, administration, faculty, staff, alumni, students, parents, and donors slug it out in the parking lot (and I do mean literally). SR-Student Recruitment was in shambles. Students have no interest in attending an organization that might not be around to give credibility to their degrees—if they could even finish them. FR-Fund-raising was difficult at best. Donors of every giving category ran away from us. Major donors are way too intelligent, frugal, and wise to waste good money on a bad investment.

I needed a way to share our new direction, mend fences, and let donors and friends know that, if they would help us survive, we would be much more wise the next round. Our first donor briefings started that fall. We asked everyone who knew and loved the college to help us recruit a friend to come and hear our story. We held sixty-five events over the next sixteen months, averaging one a week. We focused each event around a circle of friends, the largest with around sixty people and the smallest with just six people (three couples). Understand, relationships are key to helping you build and grow your major-donor program. These events were relationship-orientated and decreased the Romance time for even first-time contacts because a friend invited them to attend the briefing. Our briefings did not ask for money or a commitment in the home.

> *I encourage everyone to do a major-donor briefing at least once a quarter...*

We asked each couple or individual giving unit for the opportunity to visit them in person over the next few hours, days, or weeks. As much as possible, when it was a breakfast briefing, follow-up appointments by the college president and a volunteer were scheduled for later that same day. For evening events, follow-up appointments were scheduled for the next day whenever possible.

By no means did we pioneer this type of event. We have, however, spent considerable time perfecting the process. I encourage everyone to do a major-donor briefing at least once a quarter and more often if you have the volunteers and staff to pull it off. Events will keep you working with new donor prospects and suspects, and allow you to continue to involve your trustee board and volunteers in the process. We have held similar events all over the U.S.A., Canada, and the U.K. The bottom line is that positive peer pressure works, and people will attend if a personal friend invites them.

Personal Follow Up Makes It Work

Why do we not make a request for money or a commitment at the event? Simple. If we asked at the event, we would only get tipped. If this is the first introduction to your organization, it is very likely that a first-time gift would be $100-$500 or less. You have the greatest opportunity to ask and to network with donors if you are with them in person, one on one.

Suppose a donor attends an event or briefing, writes you a check for $5,000, and you thank him or her but do not take the time to follow up in person. This donor could be the decision-maker for a local foundation! You discover these gems by being in their homes or offices as quickly after the event as possible to begin building that relationship.

One last, very practical reason you should not ask for money or a commitment during a briefing is because the host couple is often very uncomfortable with that. Most feel that an ask in their home somehow has a bait-and-switch feel to it. The post-event, personal follow-up strategy is almost always preferred by the hosts. In the personal follow up, you can ask for bigger dollars, ask about other funding sources, and ask the ultimate question in my opinion: "Would you be open to hosting an event like this sometime in the next three to six months?" If at the event you took the money or the commitment and ran, you would miss out on the greater opportunity. Personal contact is almost always the fastest way to gather that and other important information from new major-donor contacts.

The following brief four-week calendar will help you as you define the issues leading up to an event and briefly discuss a follow-up plan.

DAY	**ACTIVITY**
Day 1	•Identify potential Briefing Host prospects. •Establish tentative date(s) for the Briefing.
Day 2	•Call Briefing Host prospects to set appointments for personal visits to recruit their involvement.
Days 4-7	•By no later than day 7, complete the personal recruitment interview with all host prospects. The interview should contain the following elements: –Thanks for previous financial involvement. –Statement of ministry direction and growth plans. –Description of Briefing, purpose, style, size, goal, etc. –Request for commitment to bring 4 to 6 indi-

viduals to the Briefing.

–Review of invitation process:
- Personal invitation by host
- Reservation commitment communicated by host to ministry no later than 7 days before the Briefing
- Letter of confirmation from ministry
- Phoned reminder from host the night before the Briefing

–Request for possible involvement of host in follow-up calls.

–Confirm date and place at each host interview.

Day 14 • Call hosts to check on progress of invitations. Remind them of reservation deadline in one week.

Day 21 • Call host (*if they have not called in*) to receive reservation confirmations.
• Mail confirmation letters to all guests.

Day 23 • Refine and confirm detailed program.
• Prepare name tags for all who will be at the Briefing.

Day 28 • Arrive at least one hour before the Briefing to set up media equipment. Be totally free of last minute details at least 1/2 hour before the Briefing to allow time to relax and greet guests.
• Confirm time assignments to each program participant.
• Get to know the name of each guest.

Personal Contact— Friend-Raising/Fund-Raising

All the mail and events in the world will not do what a personal contact can accomplish in a brief face-to-face meeting. When one of your major donors calls a friend and invites him or her to breakfast, lunch, dinner, or Starbucks to meet you, this is by far the most effective form of Recruitment. Even more effective than the group briefing, a small intimate session is where they can ask specific questions and get to know you, your ministry, CEO, or president. Your donor friend is placing the "Good Housekeeping Seal of Approval" on you and your organization. They are saying to their friend, "I believe so much in this organization, their mission, and the way they accomplish that mission, that I am proud to introduce them to you." They are essentially saying, "I believe my past financial gifts have been used effectively, and I am inviting you to consider being involved as well." I truly believe this is the ultimate test of any relationship, if donors believe in you to the point that they will encourage their friends to carefully and prayerfully consider an investment.

Alticor and many effective multi-level organizations have been built just this same way, friends in-

> *All the mail and events in the world will not do what a personal contact can accomplish in a brief face-to-face meeting.*

135

viting friends to take a look. It's called friend-raising. When you really think about it, the early church was a multi-level organization essentially started by Jesus and Peter, James, and John. The book of Acts also has a very similar friend-raising component as the early church began to mature and branch out around the region and world. Recruit your major donors and ultimately their friends to help you broaden your base of support with other major donors.

Discover Your "Pat Answers" To These Thought-Provoking Questions

1. Is there any strategy currently in place to recruit key volunteers to help your organization? How effective is the strategy and does it need to be tweaked?
2. How would you build or enhance a relationship to the point of asking one of your current major donors to help you recruit another major donor?
3. Can you name three to four individuals you would ask immediately to help you with a major-donor event?
4. Can you identify three to four locations you believe would be great for hosting a briefing?
5. Would your board members be willing to host a small group event?

8

It's All about the Stories from the Road

The task is not to get a donation, but to develop a lifelong major-donor relationship.

I believe we learn from each other, and I hope this brief overview of my past twenty-five years in the stewardship arena with major donors has been shared from a common-sense approach. Besides penning "The common thing about common sense is it ain't that common," Will Rogers is also credited for, "Every man is my teacher." I believe the statesman from Oklahoma was saying that we all have the opportunity to learn from every person with whom we come in contact over the course of our lives.

I have listened, taken copious notes, and learned a ton about life during my hundreds and hundreds of major-donor visits. I have spent time with major donors everywhere from Anchorage, Alaska, to Hong Kong, China. I have flown over three million miles while I ran a campaign for a church or organization, made an ask of a major donor, trained staff and trustees, and accomplished what the apostle Paul did with his young understudy Timothy—discipleship. Our goal at The Timothy Group is exactly that, to teach, train, do (hands on), and then to personally disciple those on the team so they can do it themselves. It has been an absolute delight. Here are some stories from the road I hope inspire you to do greater things.

U.K. Fund-Raising and Friend-Raising

In 1992 I was invited to England for the first time. I spoke at Doncaster College to the national board of a ninety-year-old ministry organization. I wondered if the principles of stewardship and the fund-raising ideas and techniques we were using in the U.S.A. and Canada would work as effectively in the old country. I was definitely a bit apprehensive. They were doing some of the same things we were doing, but this particular organization was not doing personal visiting with their current donors or prospective new donors. You know by now that my recommendation was to create a "case for support" and make some personal visits. This crazy American would even accompany them on these visits. It took a while to get organized and prepare material, but I was back sixty days later to train the staff and begin visits.

At the training session, we did some role playing, practicing answering commonly asked questions. Then we determined that I would join a number of them to make visits. Toward the end of our training session a nice lad made this statement: "Pat, I am confident you know what you are doing, but you just do not understand the British culture." He went on to say, "A man's home is his castle. When he closes the big oak door at night, he will not open it again for a fund-raising visit. That may work in America, but it will not work here in the U.K." "Fine," I replied, "but are we willing to test it and come back Friday morning to share what we learned in the field during the week?" We agreed that would be our plan.

Tuesday evening, I made a call with the executive director/president of the organization. We met the couple at their home, sat at their dining room table, drank a cup of tea with milk, and shared a need for sixty thousand pounds (about $110,000 US). The funds were to be used to underwrite the cost of a worker to minister to young people. We asked them for the entire sixty thousand pounds.

The ministry director told the prospect couple the story, and I in my very Michigan accent made the funding request. The gentleman indicated they were very interested, but had a number of very pointed questions about a location that also did not have a worker. It turned out this was an area very near their business. He asked, "What would it take to also get a worker in that area?" "An additional sixty thousand pounds," the director replied. The donor then agreed to contribute 120,000 pounds if the organization would employ a worker in both areas, to which the director heartily agreed. Finally, the donor informed us how and when he would contribute the agreed-upon commitment.

As you might imagine, I could not wait for our debriefing session on Friday morning. I led with, "Apparently a man's home is his castle, but he will open it up to you and visit with you about a ministry need if you call him up and ask him to." I was not attempting to be naughty (a term the Brits love to use). I was, however, attempting to see if personal contact was truly a universal concept. Could what worked so well in America also work in other cultures? I had my answer! Since that first home stewardship visit in the U.K., I have been involved with and orchestrated many others.

Lesson learned: The power of relationships transcends culture. The 5 R's have the capacity to work anywhere, at any time. Give them a chance and experience amazing results.

A Specific Ask and Donor Research Saved the Day

To meet the specific needs of an annual fund drive for a school some years ago, we knew we needed to identify three donors who could give $50,000 each. With two donors already committed, we called on our third prospect the Monday before Thanksgiving. This donor had given

$33,000 the previous year, so we felt very secure in preparing a written proposal with an ask of $50,000. The call was just after lunch, and we were in the donor's office a few minutes early (even an hour early is better than being five minutes late!).

He walked in and sat down behind his desk, and then he immediately handed the headmaster a check and said, "Let's get this out of the way right now." I had called to set the appointment and the donor knew we were there to ask him for money for the annual/operational needs of the school. I had not, as I've advised earlier, discussed specifics, just that we would hand deliver a personalized partnership proposal. The check he gave us was not in an envelope, and we both saw that it was for $25,000. This donor/business owner proceeded to tell us all about his family and business, and that his company had set sales records eleven of the last twelve months. He took us on a company tour (as I recall he had about one hundred employees), and as we concluded the meeting he asked, "Well, gentlemen, is there anything else?" It had been a rather one-sided conversation to that point and now it was our turn. The headmaster defined the successes of the past few months and said he needed to raise one-half million dollars for the annual operating fund. It was then my turn.

The power of relationships transcends culture.

I thanked the donor for the check, but informed him that the purpose of our visit was to both update him on the ministry and show him a proposal with a request for him and his wife to consider a gift of $50,000. "You saw the check," he said. "In fact, my wife and I wrote the check at lunch today." "Ed," I said, "if we are going to hit our annual fund goal, I want to ask if you would be open to reconsidering your check today." (This was not a cold call, or a new donor, this was a long-time donor of the organization.) "Ed, is there any way you would give consideration to our proposal and need for a gift of $50,000? By the way, are you aware that your gift to the organization last year was $33,000?" He said he was not aware of that, and began to leaf through our personalized proposal with his wife's and his name on the front.

Here is how our meeting concluded. He said, "Gentlemen, I will tell you what we will do to help you out. You can either take the check for $25,000 or I will make a matching gift of $50,000 between December 1 and 31. Here is the catch, though. All the funds given to fulfill my match must be new money. If a person last year gave $500 and gives the same amount this year it cannot be a part of my match. So, gentlemen, you can take the sure $25,000 check today or start the match next week, but I will only match the new monies you raise. What would you like to do?" (What would you do?) I asked him for a week to decide, but he said, "You have until noon tomorrow!"

A board meeting was called for 7:00 a.m. the next morning. We wanted them to wrestle with our dilemma. Ben Franklin's words "a bird in the hand is worth two in the bush" played in our minds. Should we grab the money and run, or see if we could come together as a community and meet or exceed this challenge grant? That morning, after prayer and much discussion, we went back around the room, inviting the board to consider a new or upgraded gift. We totaled $12,000. So after the 12K match we were at $24,000, and we agreed to go for it. I did, however, say to the board members, "We will need your help the next thirty days as both fund-raisers and as friend-raisers. Remember, it has to be new money or money that is over and above what was given last year."

Every player from the headmaster/CEO down worked very hard. We hit a brief snag at $33,000, another at $45,000, but with three days left until the end of the year we called this donor back and told him were at $48,000 in new money! We asked, "Is $48,000 close enough to qualify for the matching gift of $50,000?" His answer was no, but he would be delighted to match the $48K. Finally, at one of the year-end basketball games, a family wrote a check for $2,500. When it was all tallied, the organization had prayed hard, worked hard, and raised nearly $53,000 in new cash and commitments. The match was granted.

If we had not approached the major donor with a specific ask (Request), with knowledge of his previous giving history (Research), what would it have cost the organization? When I sometimes share this story at national seminars, I often get the answer $25,000. The answer actually is (and you already know by now) $75,000! He had offered a check for 25K, and then the organization raised over $100,000 after the match. That's a $75,000 turnaround, a great team effort, and an excellent opportunity to see God's hand at work.

Lesson learned: Do your Research and know your major donor's giving history. Also, approach the donor (be graciously aggressive) and ask for a specific dollar amount based upon history, relationship, and your annual, capital, or endowment funding need and timing. Their business cycle and your giving cycle (right ask, right project, right time, right person) need to fit.

Luke 14 Comes to Life in a Major-Donor Request and Gift

We began a project for an organization that had broken ground three times but had never built a building on a fifty-five acre plot of land. Their fund-raising plan was to just break ground and pray. Virtually every successful capital campaign needs at least a few additional elements like a feasibility/pre-campaign study, an effective quiet phase of soliciting lead gifts, a committee of committed volunteers, and good material/ fund-raising tools. Also helpful are a clear and concise case for support, a good campaign theme and logo, a CD, a brochure, foundation/corporation proposals, and a personalized leadership proposal for major donors. Organizations don't plan to fail, they just fail to plan. Obviously there was a fair amount of organiza-

Do your Research and know your major donor's giving history.

tional frustration about this lack of planning.

A key staff member knew a mega-donor couple who was not and never had been associated with the organization. (Remember the power of the relationship.) Scotty invited this couple to take a look at the organization. The husband quickly was invited to consider a board position. In my very first meeting with this new board member and mega donor he said, "Pat, what would the organization do with a million-dollar gift?" We easily answered that question, but the next one was a bit more difficult. "What would you do with a $5 million gift?" That one had us stumbling, but our plan and case for support was sufficient to provide a good answer. We continued to warm up the relationship with lots of Romance and inclusive meetings. We met with them as a couple as often as possible.

As we readied ourselves for a real ground breaking, we knew we needed a $4,000,000 gift to really kick this project into high gear. We asked this couple and they said they needed some time to think and pray about it. I then got an interesting call. They tracked me down and pulled me out of a planning meeting for a brief conversation. Both on the phone, they asked, "Pat, are we violating Luke 14 by giving a cash gift of this size?" She said, "Pat, do you understand the concept and the nature of our question?" Let me remind you again that "Major donors ask major questions." This was a major question that needed an honest answer.

My answer was both yes and no. "Yes, I understand Luke 14," which I then read to them. *"But don't begin until you count the cost, for who would begin construction of a building without first getting estimates and then checking to see if there is enough money to pay the bills, otherwise you might complete only the foundation before running out of funds, and then how everyone would laugh at you, they would say, 'there's the person who started that building and ran out of money before it was finished.'"* (NLT)

"And yes," I continued, "I understand that a lack of planning could cause the organization another false start. No, I do not think you will help the organization become guilty of violating Luke 14, because we already know how your gift, as a leveraged match, will help us raise many additional dollars. Your gift," I explained to them, "will be an 'over the top' gift that will allow us to truly break ground and begin to see block and steel come up out of the ground. Your gift will provide the credibility this organization and the campaign needs. In fact, may we announce your gift at a sit-down dinner less than a week away? May we call a press conference to share this good news with the community regarding this anonymous gift?" To both of the questions, they replied, "yes."

The CEO did the vision pitch at the evening dinner and, toward the end, we had five young ladies come out and interrupt his speech. Of course this well-rehearsed part of the presentation became the show stopper. These five ladies indicated they were the "five miracle girls" of this organization. Each of them shared a different miracle from the past that clearly defined the unique history of the organization. The last girl brought the house down when she took the microphone and announced to the over three hundred attendees, "I am the miracle gift of $4,000,000 that will allow us to break ground and begin construction immediately."

In the past more than twenty-five years, I have attended many fund-raising dinners but nothing like this one. There was an outpouring of joy and excitement like I have never seen or experienced. I was in the audience and smiled with great joy as one man near my table stood on his chair, and then on his table, thanking and praising God. It was really incredible. The coolest part, however, was the press conference where the local paper asked twenty different ways how they could communicate with these anonymous donors (by letter, encrypted e-mail, scrambled telephone call, private instant messenger, etc.). The chief development officer finally asked them, "What part of 'no' and 'anonymous' don't you understand?" The article in the newspaper the next day listed the donors as anonymous. Hey, the press got it right for a change.

That evening the president announced the ground-breaking ceremony and asked the crowd to be the first to get it on their calendars and into their PDA's so they could attend. This couple did not violate Luke 14.

Major donors ask major questions.

Instead they helped us establish momentum and garner the credibility to move a major capital effort forward. That is the power that major/mega donors have and the profound impact they can make on an organization and, in this instance, an entire community.

One final part of this story was the Recruitment part. I spoke with the same couple about becoming friend-raisers. The man did not have the time, but he believed his wife would help. I met with her, defined the task, and asked if she would help us share the story and invite a few friends to join her in this project. She was so cute. She said, "Now, Pat, let me get this straight. I am a little old woman with money and you want me to contact other little old ladies with money, is that correct?" She got it! She was a great help in being a friend-raiser for the project.

Lesson learned: Never underestimate the power of a key relationship. Let it take you as far as possible. Work out your strategic plan and show major donors how their gifts can really make the difference. Communicate early and often with your major-donor friends. Then after the gift is given, keep them informed and recruit them to help you open additional doors in your community. Remember that the number one reason people give is because of *who* asks.

Never underestimate the power of a key relationship.

I have many success stories because the principles we have been sharing are time-tested and work. Many years ago, I began collecting these stories and statements from major donors, and these three are great examples from that lengthy list.

As I said in the Preface for this book, I am and will always remain a field person. Too many in the fund-raising field have become theorists. They can give you the theory on why you should do this or that, but have not tested it in the real place it matters—sitting at the kitchen table of a major-donor couple, helping an organization share their mission, vision, and core values and asking others to partner with them in a big way.

Now let's talk heading on to home plate and finishing strong!

It's All about Finishing Strong

*Never give up
because it ain't over till it's over.*
—Yogi Berra

Any baseball coach or player will tell you a lot of baseball games are won in the ninth inning. Both defensive and offensive teams have a strategy to close out a game. The team on defense (the ones in the field) send in their closer to ensure they get three outs and hold the lead. The team on offense (those up to bat) want to move a runner into scoring position and round third base and send him home to tie it up or win the game.

Building your major-donor strategy is similar to a base-ball game in this regard. The game is over in nine innings, but the season continues. Working with your major donors is a life-time pursuit. One project may be funded but many additional projects are on the horizon. Hence, you have a goal to finish strong and truly plan for the future. The game plan shared in this book will work if you commit yourselves to the major-donor strategy. How do I know? Because I saw it work last year, last month, and last week for organizations we are privileged to serve. Remember, I am a practitioner, and I am in the field nearly every week teaching, training, discipling, and doing. These organizations have finished strong with their major donors and have prepared themselves for the next encounter/game day with these high-capacity friends.

Back to the Future

As you already know, "penny-wise but pound-foolish" is one of my favorite British clichés. In my hundreds of conversations with clients all over the world, I have found many to be guilty of that biting British reality. Their planning has been shortsighted, they have bowed to the tyranny of the urgent, and they have not looked toward the future. They "grabbed the money and ran" when they should have been more concerned about building relationships for the future. They

> *Working with your major donors is a life-time pursuit.*

did not finish strong, they only won today's game and did not think about a game coming up next week, next month, or next year.

Readers are leaders. I encourage you to continue to read a couple of business or management books each year. A book that impacted my thoughts and consulting practice is *Good to Great* by the social scientist, corporate researcher, and former Stanford University Business School faculty member Jim Collins. He shares many insightful concepts about what companies/organizations do to take themselves from "good to great." While chapter three of his book seems to be mostly about staffing, I have a bit of an expanded perspective on Jim's thoughts. He writes about getting the right people on the bus, the wrong people off the bus, and the right people in the right seats on the bus. But here is the issue that struck me. He said, "Do all of this planning before you ever get the bus rolling." I often believed a parked bus was of no use to anyone, you had to get it moving. I now buy into the management practice of doing your planning and reshuffling before getting the bus going. Your Research and Romance phases are going to help you identify specific major donors and get them in the right seat (their area of interest and passion).

Back to our Research chapter, major donors often buy into organizational needs that surround programs, personnel, or property. The 3 P's of planning help you discover their specific area of mission, their vision, and the core values that drive their giving patterns. Remember, most major donors do not want to help you fund the past or the present, they want to help you purchase and ensure the future. These donors have been successful in their business and personal lives because they always take a brief look back (what got us here) but are always looking ahead (where we want to finish). They have embraced their existing reality but know they must go back to the future and implement their vision to finish strong. Jim Collins and many others continue to confirm the importance of planning. The future is sometimes defined by what we do today.

This concept was secured in my mind and heart in a recent meeting with a former commandant of the United States Marine Corps. This retired four star general made this profound statement: "As a member of the joint chiefs of staff of this nation it was my job to oversee the Corps today but to plan for ten years ahead." I truly believe this is the role of CEO's/ presidents/trustee boards and members of the advancement/development staff. At the end of this particular game we want to round third and step on home plate. But there is another game, tomorrow and ten years from now. Plan your work...then work your plan. This is the only way to achieve long-term success. You always want to briefly look back but really take a good hard look forward. When we create a case statement or the script for a DVD for a campaign or project, we use 5 percent of the document to define the past (organizational history) and use 40-50 percent to define the vision for the future. Al-

The future is sometimes defined by what we do today.

ways envision and clearly define the future of your organization in your major-donor strategy.

Volunteers Can Help You Win the Game

It is no great secret that staff people in the business and corporate world are being asked daily to do more with less. It is no doubt the same with your advancement/development team. You are conducting a comprehensive campaign for annual, capital, and endowment funds, and you have too few staff to accomplish the task. But a key to your future success may well be within your reach—volunteers!

It is also no secret that the last decade has proven it is easier to ask a volunteer for money than for time. In our modern society where technology has supposedly helped us cut corners and find more time, we all seem to be busier than ever. It takes eight to ten minutes to bake a potato in a microwave, not the forty-five minutes it used to take when we used a conventional oven. We can check our e-mails on the fly since we no longer have to sit at a computer because of wireless connections. But we all still seem way too busy, certainly too busy to volunteer our most precious possession—our time. Technology has certainly impacted our lives for the positive but high-tech will not take the place of relationships. Regardless of how high-tech you have become, remember to be high-touch. And volunteers are a key component to help you build and finish strong with your major-donor program.

An organization recently told me they are trying to get

all of their work done with volunteers. But they also indicated they think it takes more time to recruit, train, and manage their volunteers than the value they receive from those relationships. Wow, is that your perspective on volunteerism in your organization? I hope not! In my more than twenty-five years of serving all kinds of organizations I have become convinced there are three kinds of volunteers: Shirkers, Jerkers, and Workers.

Shirkers are those who never agree to do anything for their favorite charity. They just changed jobs or they are uncomfortable sharing names or it is a conflict of interest...or something. They find clever ways to shirk any and

Volunteers Can Help You Win the Game

all responsibilities for your organization. I am certain some avoid volunteerism for legitimate reasons, but many just choose not to serve. They are so caught up in themselves and their busy schedules that they just can't find or spare the time.

Jerkers may be a new term to you but one I think is legitimate based upon my years of experience. Jerkers agree to serve and start out with high energy and enthusiasm but fairly quickly drop out of the volunteer process. They talk a great line but are often unable to perform at your level of expectation, or any level for that matter. Or they say yes, yes, yes until the real work or "heavy lifting" of the effort and time commitments are defined. They are great starters but for a variety of reasons are unable to finish the ball game. Most base-

...the last decade has proven it is easier to ask a volunteer for money than for time.

ball managers want their starters to pitch into the fifth or sixth inning and, if possible, into the seventh or eighth. If a pitcher consistently can only go one or two innings (a Jerker) their time with the ball club will be short. They are more than likely on their way back to the minor leagues. Are you weary of minor league volunteers? Then step up to the plate and recruit my third designation of volunteer—Workers.

Workers are the major leaguers. If you recruit and train them and invite them to buy into your mission with their time, talent, and treasure, you will have a long-term Worker. If they agree to make eight to ten major donor visits with you or a board or campaign team member, they get it done and do it with a sense of purpose.

If the number one reason people give to an organization for the first time or in a big way is because of who asks, it is imperative that you recruit volunteers who are Workers. These key volunteers become networkers and help you open doors of opportunity that you could never open on your own or with your existing staff. Develop your own volunteer team composed of Workers. Your organization will begin to win today and certainly develop a team to make an impact on the future.

My friend Steve Wilson and I worked on a capital project nine times the size of the largest previous campaign in the history of Lakeland Christian School. In conversation about our major donor/quiet phase of the campaign, Steve made this profound comment. He said, "Pat, in addition to a good plan, great material, and a passionate case for support, we have recruited a campaign committee of over fifty people who are winners. These volunteers are effective leaders who will help us finish strong because that is part of their DNA. They are winners!" These volunteers have placed their personal and professional reputation on the line with Steve and Dr. Mike Sligh and other leaders at the school. Their names are in print in the campaign material, and if we fail to achieve our goal they have also failed. But these folks are not about failing at anything. Their leadership, passion, abilities, and resources will help us be successful. Now you answer the question, do you really want to conduct a campaign/major donor effort without the wise counsel, networking ability, and resources of your key volunteers?

Here's one final word on volunteerism in America, Canada, and the U.K. I have heard the term *FAT*

> *You want volunteers who are already donors to your organization and have proved their faithfulness.*

used in relationship to your volunteers. FAT is an acrostic for Faithful, Accessible, and Teachable. Think about it for a second. You want volunteers who are already donors to your organization and have proved their faithfulness. You are not trying to convince them of anything, they are already sold on the organization. They have clearly demonstrated their faithfulness by years of activity or an intense desire to become involved and help you move forward. Keep in mind these faithful volunteers may be in the first or second round of investing time with your organization.

Accessibility is also critical since people tend to do exactly what they want to do with their time, talent, and treasure. When a volunteer says to you, "I do not have time to help out with your major donor effort," what they are really saying is, "That project is just not high enough on my priority list to warrant that investment of my time." As you Recruit and Romance your volunteers, it is key to also enroll them as donors. "If your treasure is there so will your heart be also" is a great quote from Matthew 6:21. If you get their treasure you are well on the way to getting their hearts, and with their hearts comes an investment of time.

Your volunteers must be accessible and willing to do what you ask them to do when you need it done.

The third letter in the acrostic is T for Teachable. Now that sounds silly. What can you and I teach a corporate executive or very successful professional person in this volunteer process? We can teach them a ton, and I mean a ton. With volunteers in a major-donor effort we are not looking for slick sales people, but you can teach them how to share your story with passion. And you can create a tool to help them with the Request (the ask). I continue to be amazed at the number of corporate and professional people who routinely close million-dollar deals but cannot ask their best friend for a dollar let alone $10,000 for your organization without some teaching and training. Yes, I am talking about a prepared script and role playing for those who are going to become a part of your volunteer network. Provide them with a job description and clear expectations. It is worth repeating: "Volunteers do what we inspect, not what we expect." You may even need to join them on a few calls so they get it right. Recruit volunteers with a teachable spirit. Remember, sometimes you have not because you ask not. Recruit a teachable volunteer base and then teach them. This is critical to helping you finish strong.

Ask in Their Area of Passion, but Remember to Ask

Allow me to remind all of you again about the importance of the ask. Many major donors do not give because there is no follow up, and most of all because there is no ask. We have inherited a capital/major donor project with a follow-up problem. Letters were sent out six to nine months ago, inviting the potential major-donor prospect to welcome a telephone call and a personal visit in the next thirty to sixty days. Apparently they had identified their area of passion but had forgotten to ask. How do you think we will do when we attempt to breathe new life into this campaign? I can assure you, since there are no do-overs (remember chapter 1), we are going to need to mend some fences and re-establish some relationships.

The ask/Request is not a faucet you can turn on and off when you want or need something. The ask is not manipulation; that flat out will not work. It is not about heavenly hinting, that beating-about-the-bush meeting. It is not a surprise. Your major-donor prospect knows your visit is about making a request for partnership. It is not a cold call, so you cannot sneak up on them. And this is more than likely not your first visit (although, with good volunteer input, you can get to third and perhaps home in a short period of time).

The ask/Request is a partnership meeting, the merging of your values and theirs. If it fits it is an eternal investment. The ask is a specific invitation, providing a range of giving to help them make a true stewardship decision. The ask is visionary. It may address the present but must also help address the future for your organization. It is professional but not slick. It is a bold request—clear, compelling, and results-based. Most of all, enjoy this unique interaction with your high-capacity friends and donors.

Here is some real additional field research on this topic. In another project in California we had a board chairperson who was a wonderful

Take the time to discover the area of passion of your major donors...

leader and was also a fundraising volunteer we had helped along in the process. He rated a good friend and business leader in that city as having the capacity to give $250,000 over a three-year period. This friend certainly qualified as a major-donor prospect. The board chair promised me he would visit his friend and make the ask prior to a fall sit-down dinner to announce commitments to date and kick off the campaign. I even went so far as to script a telephone call inviting those handful of people we had been attempting to visit to not make a commitment at the dinner but allow us to visit them after the event. We did not want them to "tip" us but to consider a true stewardship decision.

The donor in question showed up at the dinner and made a written commitment that evening of $90,000. He agreed to give $30,000 a year for three years and wrote the first check and included it in the envelope provided at the dinner. Imagine the dilemma. We had received a very generous gift but it was not the one we had intended to ask the donor to consider. The board chairperson placed us in a tough spot because he failed to ask in a timely manner as promised, and a group ask is always less effective than a personal request. How do you go back and start over when we all know by now there are no do-overs?

An administrator of a college preparatory school with tuition in the neighborhood of $10,000 a year made an incredible statement a few months ago. He said, "It took me five years to raise money to complete our library/technology/media center and one afternoon to raise the money for our football stadium, press box, and concession area." While I believe his statement was somewhat tongue in cheek, it made a strong point. Here is a K-12 school sending students to Ivy League colleges, military academies, and the like, and you would think his results would have been just the opposite: Five years to raise money for athletics and one afternoon to fund and enhance their academic prowess. Like it or not, we are a society driven by sports, and this is exactly what the administrator was defining.

I once had a major donor who had just made a $500,000 commitment to a Christian school say, "If I thought the school was more about academics than sports I would double the size of my gift." We quickly got back with him and took along some fine students both in person and on video tape and showcased the academic quality of the school. We had him interview students who were at or near the top of the student body of colleges they were attending. One student mentioned he tested out of calculus and had the fifth highest grade of the four hundred freshmen who took that advanced math exam. The student shared with the donor that he felt well prepared for the rigors of college because of the academic program at his private Christian high school. The donor doubled his gift. His area of interest was academics and he gave significantly because of that area of interest. Take the time to discover the area of passion of your major donors in your Research and Romance phases, then be faithful to make the Request (ask). By doing so, you will get a gift for this project and begin to pave the way for partnership in the future. This is the process for finishing strong.

It is no secret that stewards who are mature both in age and in their understanding of the process make great major/mega donor prospects. Grandparents love to give to causes that involve their grandchildren. Follow that level of passion with grandparents back to their children and grandchildren. Those relationships have built-in passion because of the relationships and they make for instant major-donor prospects and suspects.

Here is a final ask/Request checklist:

WHO .... The Right Prospect—Researched, Romanced, and Ready

WHAT .... The Right Project—The right gift request

WHEN .... The Right Time—For them and for your organization

WHERE ...... The Right Place—Their kitchen or office table

WHY .... The Right Person—#1 reason people say yes to a Request

Blueprint for Success: A Winning Game Plan

You must establish a major-donor attitude from top to bottom in your organization. This includes the person who answers the phone (and even your telephone system needs to be easy to navigate). One organization recently moved a staff person who was unfriendly and a bit mean-spirited out of the front office and off the telephone. What if a major donor called with a question about a stock transfer or dividend payment or whatever and was treated rudely? Months and years of good Research and Romance can go down the drain very quickly.

A written plan and major-donor strategy complete with dollar values attached to every project is key. What is it you need to raise, what will it accomplish, and how will the donor's gift today make an impact immediately, tomorrow, and in the future? The donor asks questions to see if you pass the test. Planning will prevent that deer-in-the-headlight stare. A donor asked us on the first visit, "What would you do with a $1 million gift today?" His next question after being satisfied with our answer was, "What would you do with a $5 million gift today?" A written plan will help you define those issues in advance. Remember, no do-overs. Also remember, Yogi Berra defined it best when he said "If you don't know where you are going you are liable to end up someplace else."

CEO and board of trustee ownership is critical to the success of your major-donor program. One more time in case you missed it, the number-one fund-raiser in your organization is your CEO, president, the boss. By now you know that's because many major donors want to meet with the CEO. We are often asked who the CEO is and who is on the board. Just a few weeks ago a major donor asked us, "Who is on the board and who is leading this campaign effort?" He was sizing us up by who was leading the effort. Just like Steve Wilson's team of winners, this foundation director in his seventies wanted to be sure his investment was secure and the project would come to fulfillment. Board members serve a number of functions. See if you can remember these 5 G's:

➤ Godly leadership
➤ Governors (They make polity and policy decisions)
➤ Givers (They invest their personal financial resources in the organization)
➤ Get (Others to give they are networkers)
➤ Get Off (Does that sound harsh? I hope not. That is not my intent.)

These 5 G's will change the way your board does business. Getting them involved will help you broaden your base of support and open new doors with major donors. Your CEO and your board can have a significant impact on your major-donor game plan.

Please, please, please do not forget that final touch. Everyone is high-tech. We can do "hard asset" research, donor demographics, and psychographics. We can analyze giving patterns every which way from Sunday. But don't forget high-touch. Don't forget to visit your major donors and call them and love them and spend quality time with them. Don't forget the handwritten notes and birthdays and anniversaries and little acts of kindness you do for others you love. See the people, see the people, see the people is a lost art these days. Winning the game is not about rocket science; it is *all about relationships.*

Case in point, a story that has been shared many times at a Wesleyan Methodist college here in America is about one of their very wealthy donors. The man moved away from the college area and somehow everyone on the advancement staff and even the president figured, "Oh well, he has been our friend forever and will be to the end." Well, the end came and, much to their surprise, 90 percent of the large estate went to a Catholic organization that had built a short-term relationship late in this donor's life. They had forgotten to maintain their level of high-touch. They thought it was in the bag so to speak, but it obviously was not.

> *Winning the game is not about rocket science; it is all about relationships.*

Runs Only Count if You Touch Home Plate

An announcer will conclude a half inning of baseball in this way: "No runs on two hits and two men left on base and at the end of six innings it is the donors 2 and the advancement team 0."

Runs do not count no matter how close you get unless the runners step on home plate. You have to touch all the bases, round third base, and head for home. Getting close in a major-donor program does not always count, and it certainly did not work for the college we just mentioned. Now I understand there is another day, another game, another opportunity. But at some point those opportunities come to an end. Yes, I understand the planned giving/estate planning process, but that is another book, not this one. You must help major-donor prospects enjoy the moment and help you touch home plate and score for the many people you will be able to serve with their gifts.

Get out of your office and see your major-donor prospects and suspects in person. Pay for a plane trip to sit at their kitchen tables and drink cups of tea and tell them how their partnership in the past has been helpful and how their gifts in the future could help. Network, network, network. Ask them who else they know who could help your organization with a gift.

Make sure the right person is along to help you build the relationship and to make the initial ask. Be specific with that ask, be firm but fair and be specific. I have always believed we may have asked too low if the donor did not gasp a bit. Don't be foolish but be bold and confident.

Do great follow up, say thanks, and really mean it. Go the extra mile to say thanks in person and personally update them on the difference their gifts made. Last but not least, recruit them to help you as friend-raisers. Many major donors abhor the idea of becoming a fund-raiser but they often welcome the opportunity to become a friend-raiser.

Now go do it! Yes, it is hard work. Yes, you may fail a time or two. Yes, it can be a bit intimidating. But I believe in it because I have seen it work hundreds and hundreds of times. I believe a well-managed major-donor program is the most cost-effective way to raise money. Bigger dollars add up faster and one or two major donor gifts can do as much or more than your entire year of direct mail, more than your auction and fund-raising dinner combined.

It is the bottom of the ninth inning and now it's your time to shine. You have walked the major-donor prospect through the right steps. That's the good news. But even better news

> *Do great follow up, say thanks, and really mean it.*

is that if this is not the right game for them, there is always tomorrow or the next day. In fact, there are over 250 billion reasons to establish a major-donor game plan as we here in America have surpassed the $250 billion barrier in annual philanthropic giving in the past year. The joy on the face and in the heart of your major donors as they round third and touch home to help you win today and tomorrow is worth every inning of hard work. Now, play ball!

To purchase additional copies of this book, or for more information on how to receive an organizational or quantity discount, go to www.timothygroup.com or contact The Timothy Group at 616-224-4060.